Amherstburg Ontario Book 1 in Colour Photos, Saving Our History One Photo at a Time

Photography
by Barbara Raué
2015

Series Name:
Cruising Ontario

Book 120: Amherstburg Book 1

Cover photo: 210 Dalhousie Street

Series Name: Cruising Ontario
Saving Our History One Photo at a Time
in colour photos

Books Available in Alphabetical Order:

Aberfoyle, Acton, Alton, Ancaster, Arthur, Aylmer, Ayr, Bloomingdale, Brantford, Burlington, Caledon, Caledonia, Cambridge, Clifford, Conestogo, Delhi, Dorchester to Aylmer, Drayton, Drumbo, Dundas, Eden Mills, Elmira, Elora, Fergus, Guelph, Hagersville, Hamilton, Hanover, Harriston, Hespeler, Jarvis, Kitchener, Linwood, Listowel, London, Lucknow, Mono, Mount Forest, Neustadt, New Hamburg, Niagara-on-the-Lake, Oakville, Orangeville, Orillia, Owen Sound, Palmerston, Peterborough, Port Elgin, Preston, Rockwood, Seaforth, Sheffield, Shelburne, Simcoe, Southampton, St. Jacobs, St. Thomas, Stoney Creek, Stratford, Tillsonburg, Waterdown, Waterrford, Waterloo, Wellesley, Wingham

Other Books by Barbara Raue

Coins of Gold

Arrows, Indians and Love

The Life and Times of Barbara
Volume 1: Inventions That Have Enhanced My Life
Volume 2: Entertainment That I Have Enjoyed
Volume 3: East Coast Trips
Volume 4: Olympics Have Always Intrigued Me
Volume 5: Wonders of the World
Volume 6: Caribbean Cruises We Have Enjoyed
Volume 7: Animals
Volume 8: Storms and Other Major Disasters in My Lifetime
Volume 9: Wars, Terrorist Attacks and Major Disasters

The Cromwell Family Book

Laura Secord Discovered

Daddy Where Are You?

Visit Barbara's website to view all of her books
http://barbararaue.ca

Table of Contents

Amherstburg is located near the mouth of the Detroit River in Essex County about twenty-five kilometres south of the United States city of Detroit, Michigan. The British military garrison, Fort Malden, was established here in 1796. The town was developed by Loyalists who were granted land by the Crown in Ontario after the British lost the American Revolutionary War. The Loyalists built many of their houses in the French style of a century before, giving the new town a historic character.

The local public high school in Amherstburg is General Amherst High School and is named after Jeffery Amherst, 1st Baron Amherst of Montreal, who served as an officer in the British Army and as Commander-in-Chief of the Forces. Amherst is best known as the architect of Britain's successful campaign to conquer the territory of New France during the French and Indian War when he led the British attack on Louisbourg on Cape Breton Island in June 1758. Amherst led an army against French troops on Lake Champlain, where he captured Fort Ticonderoga in July 1759, while another army under Sir William Johnson took Niagara also in July 1759, and James Wolfe besieged and eventually captured Quebec with a third army in September 1759.

From July 1760, Amherst led an army down the St. Lawrence River from Fort Oswego, joined with Brigadier Murray from Quebec and Brigadier Haviland from Ill-aux-Noix in a three-way pincer, and captured Montreal, ending French rule in North America on September 8. In recognition of this victory, Amherst was appointed as the first British Governor General in the territories that eventually became Canada.

From his base at New York, Amherst oversaw the dispatch of troops under Monckton and Haviland to take part in British expeditions in the West Indies that led to the British capture of Dominica in 1761 and Martinique and Cuba in 1762.

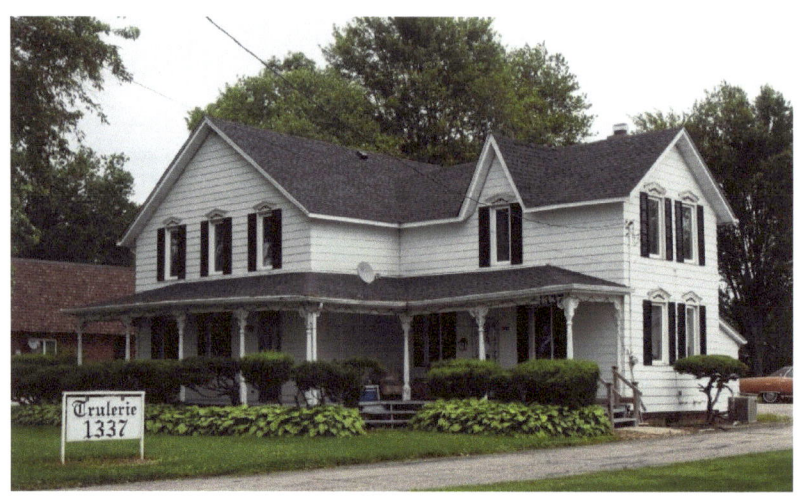
1337 Dalhousie Street

Simon Girty (1741-1818)

Girty's life crossed cultural boundaries between native and white societies of the frontier of American settlement in 1756. His family was captured by a French-led native war party in Pennsylvania. Simon was adopted by the Seneca, and then repatriated in 1764. An interpreter at Fort Pitt (Pittsburgh), he became an intermediary with native nations. In 1778, dismayed over rebel policy on the native, Girty fled to Detroit. During the Revolutionary War and subsequent conflicts in the Ohio valley, he was employed by the British Indian Department while serving native nations as a negotiator, scout, and military leader. Angry at his defection and fearful of his influence, Americans made Girty a scapegoat for frontier atrocities. He is buried here on his homestead.

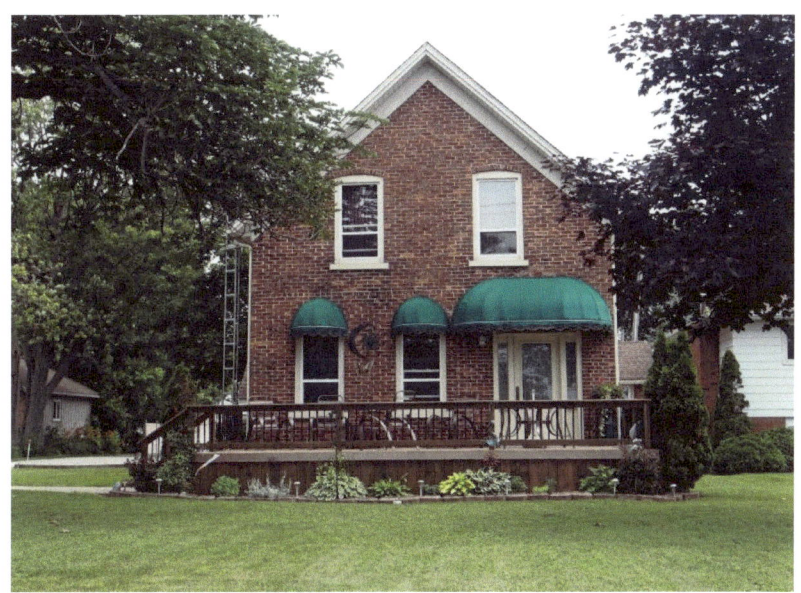

Dalhousie Street - Gothic

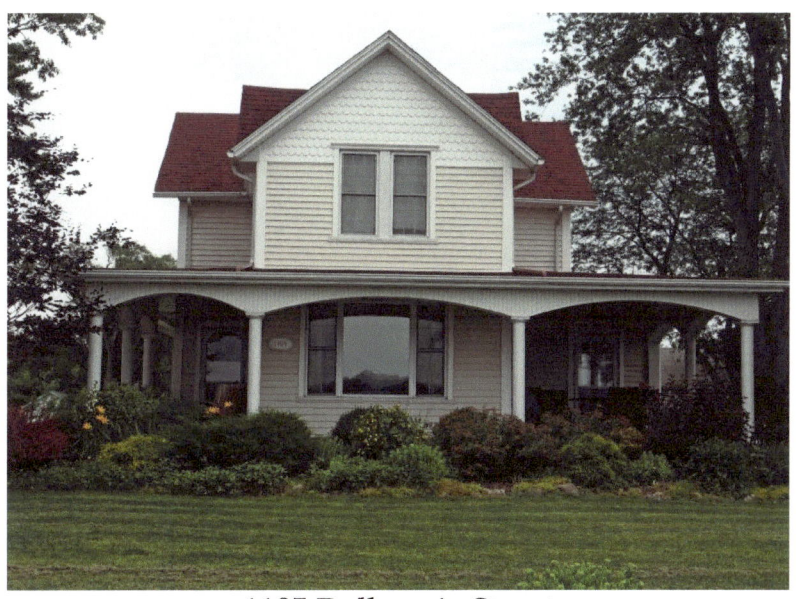

1105 Dalhousie Street

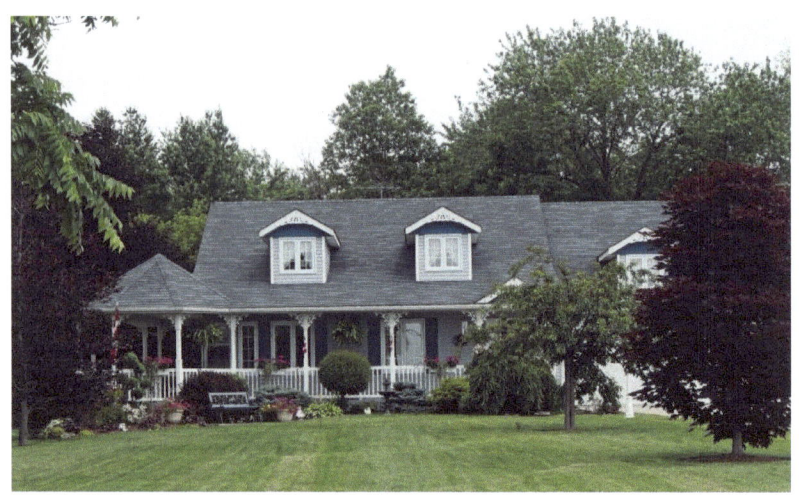

Dalhousie Street – dormers in attic

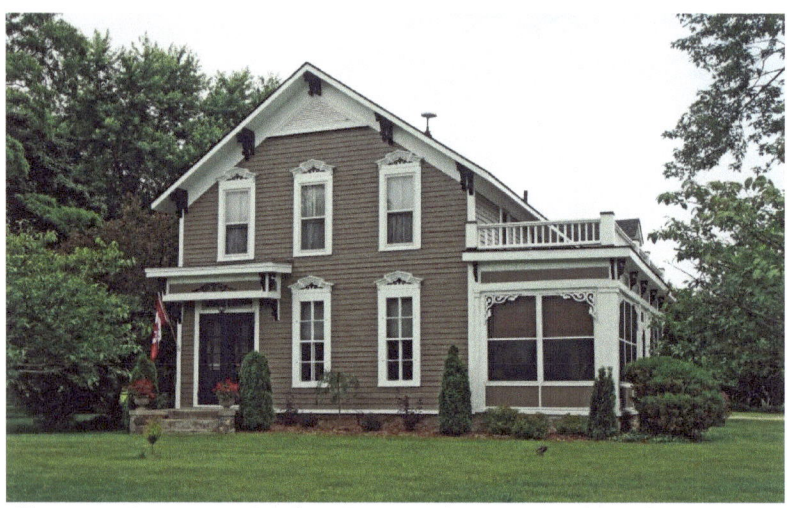

Dalhousie Street – Gothic Revival, cornice brackets, second floor balcony, window hoods, transom window above door, fancy wood scrollwork on window hoods and window frames

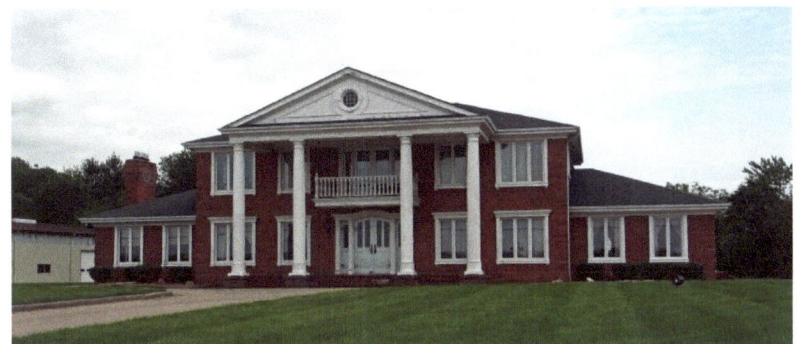

Dalhousie Street – Greek Revival, two-storey Doric pillars, pediment, second floor balcony, side lights beside door

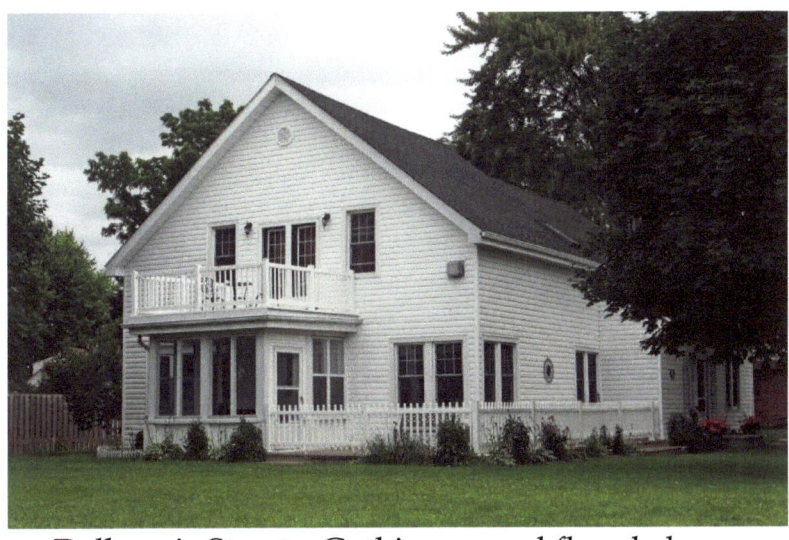

Dalhousie Street – Gothic - second floor balcony

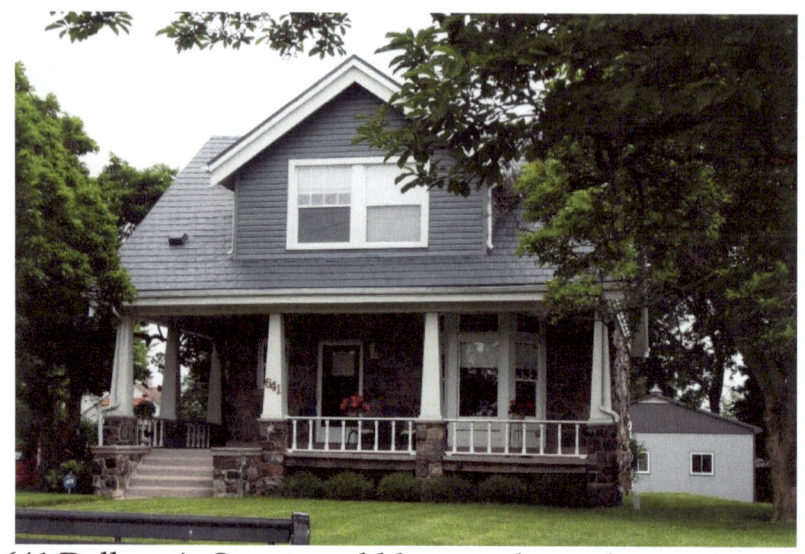

641 Dalhousie Street – cobblestone, large dormer in attic

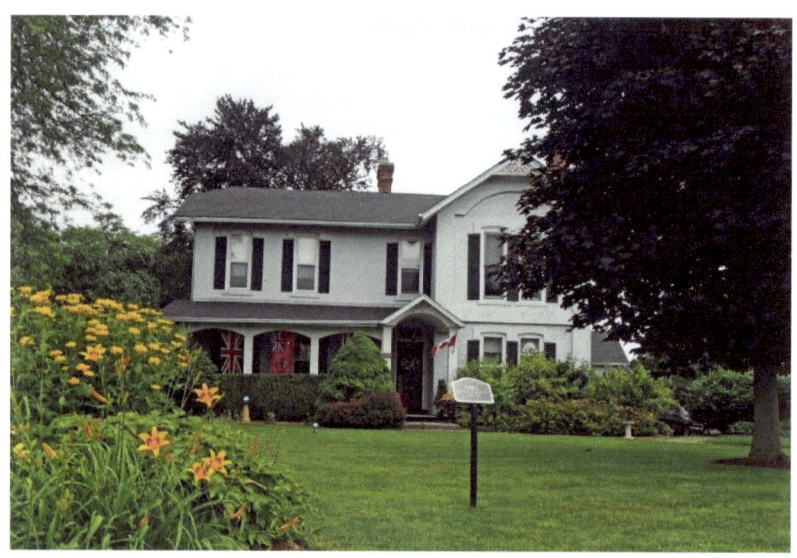

Dalhousie Street – Boyle/Smith House – 1882
Bargeboard trim on gable

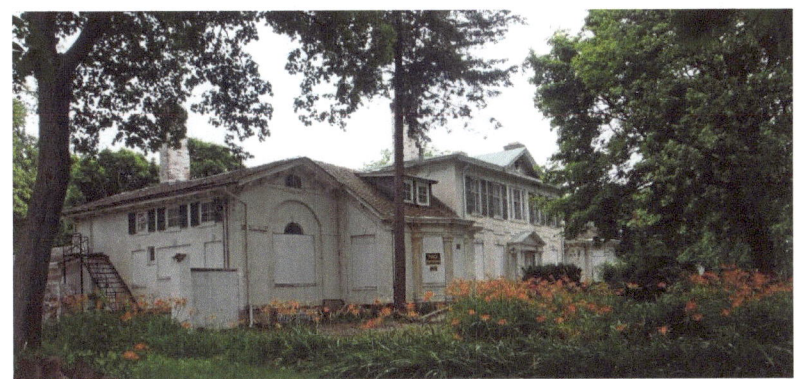

Palladian Architecture – central core with a wing on each side; hipped roof, symmetrical front of central section are evidence of British Classicism – 23 rooms

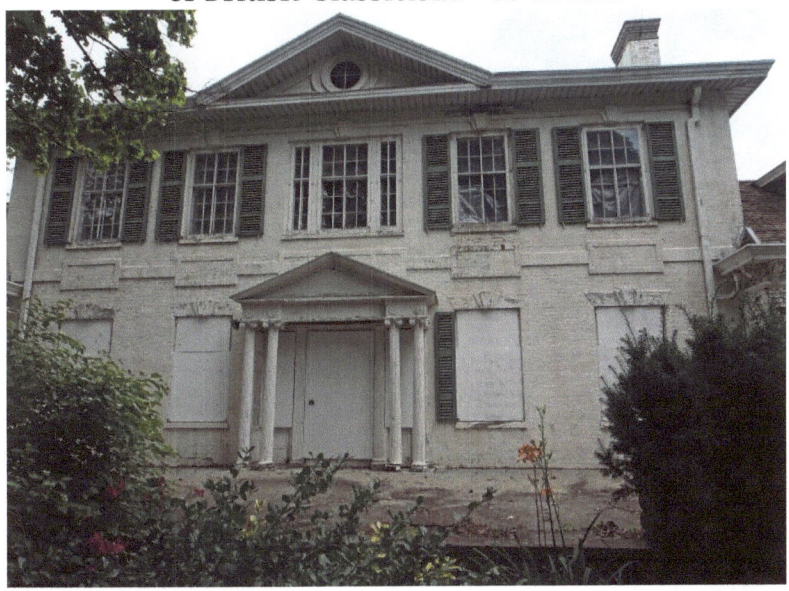

525 Dalhousie Street - Bellevue House – 1816-1819

One of the finest remaining examples of domestic Georgian Neo-Classical architecture in Ontario – the home of Robert Reynolds, the commissary to the garrison at Fort Malden, and his sister, Catherine Reynolds, an accomplished landscape painter who worked in pencil, crayon, sepia wash and water colours recording scenes along the Detroit River and Lake Erie

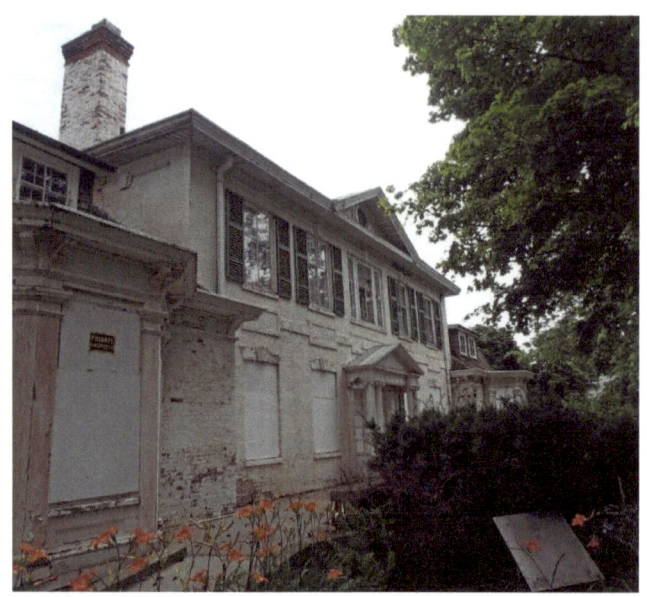

Large central hipped roof with gabled dependencies - imposing chimneys, columns with Ionic capitals capped by a pediment above the door, dentil moulding

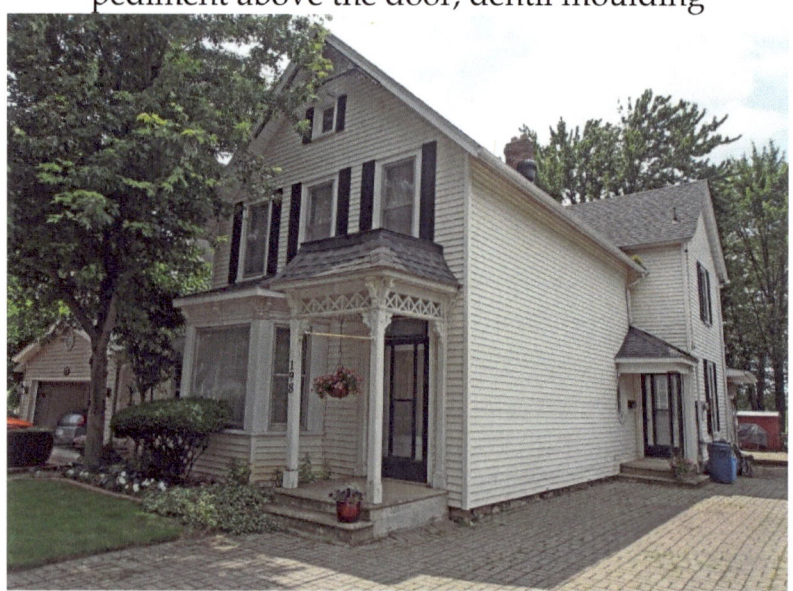

198 Dalhousie Street – Gothic Revival – verge board trim on gable

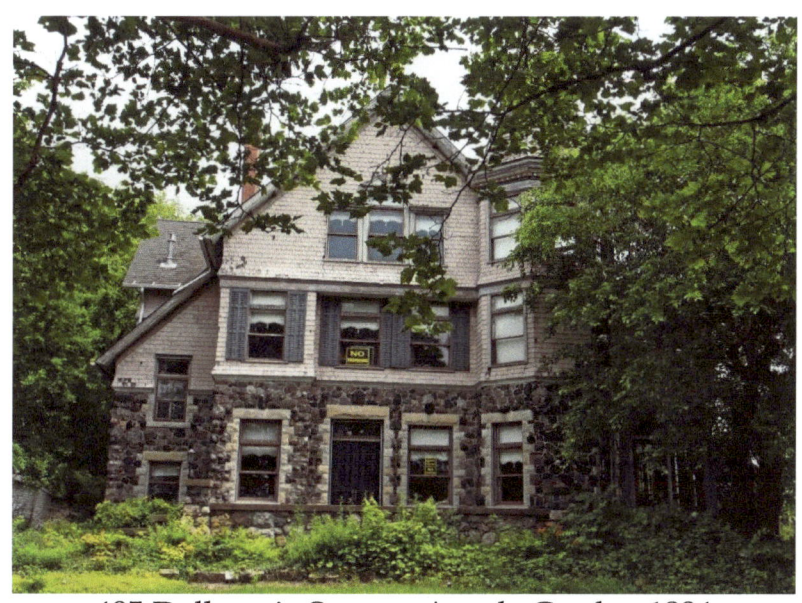

495 Dalhousie Street – Argyle Castle - 1894
Arts and Crafts style, Palladian style window with
window hood, turret

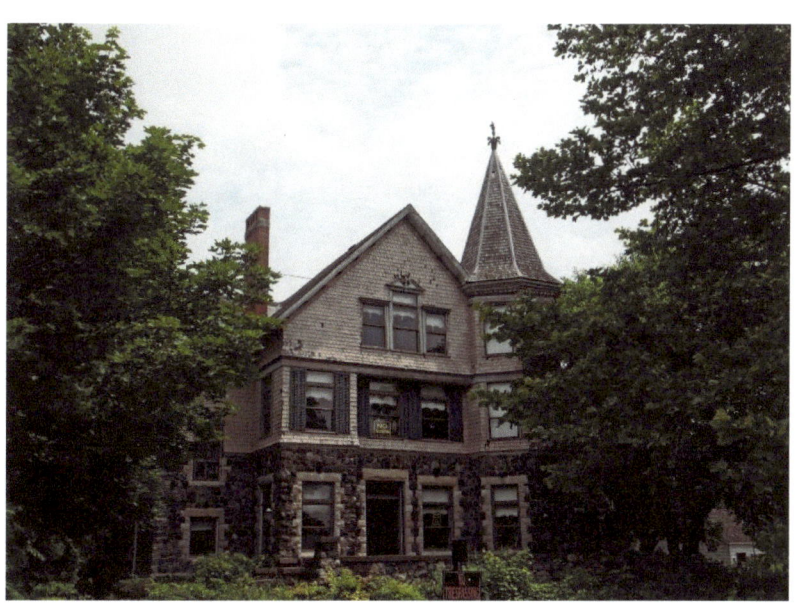

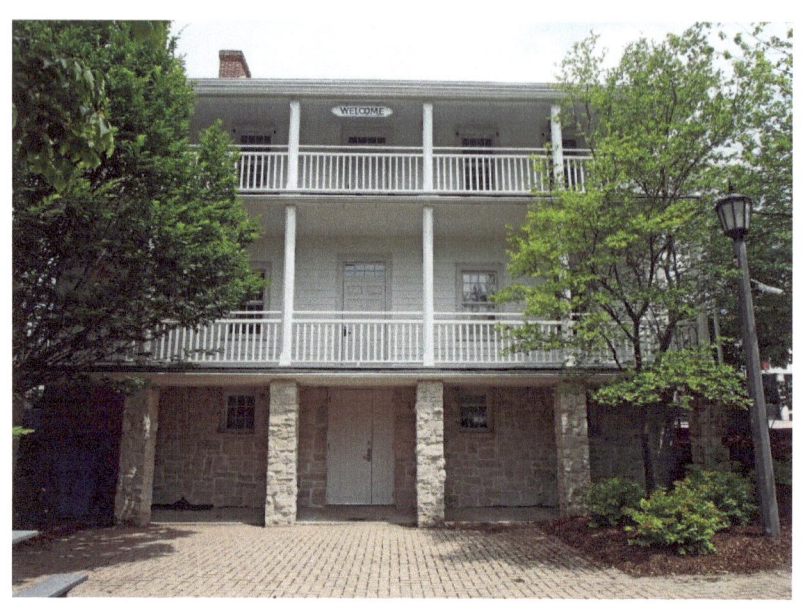

268 Dalhousie Street

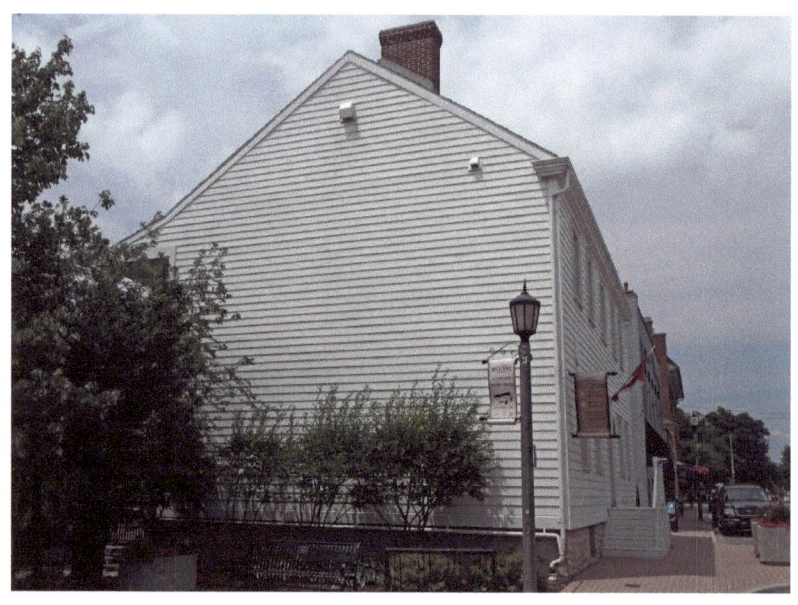

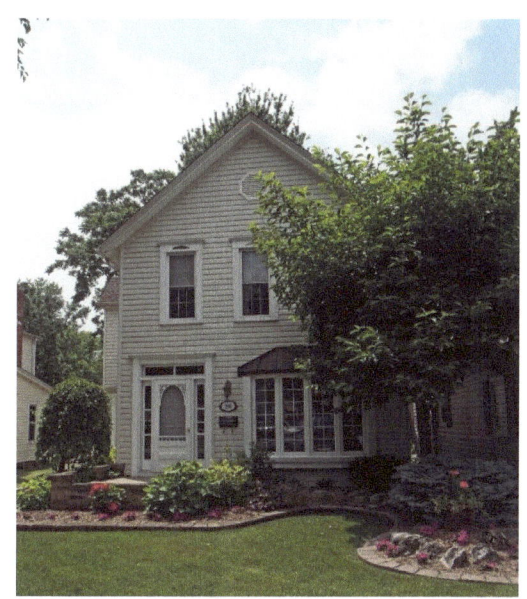

206 Dalhousie Street – Gothic Revival

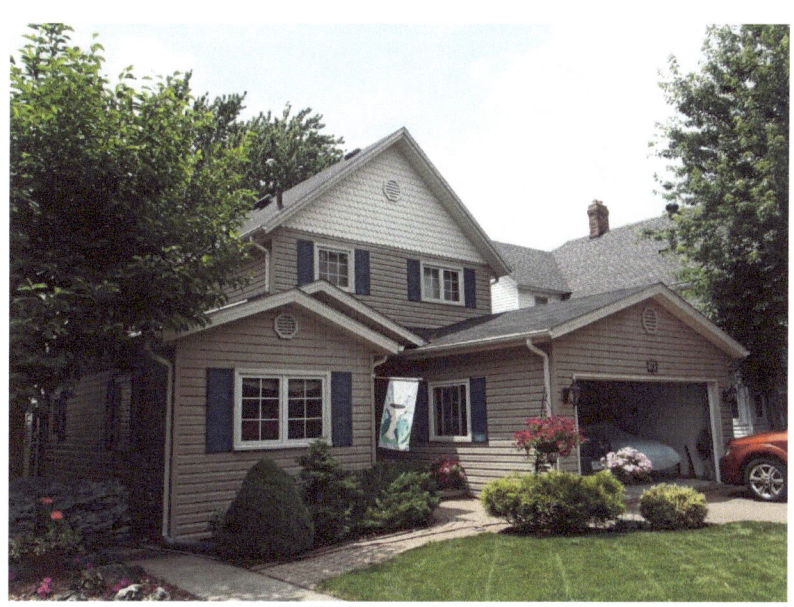

202 Dalhousie Street

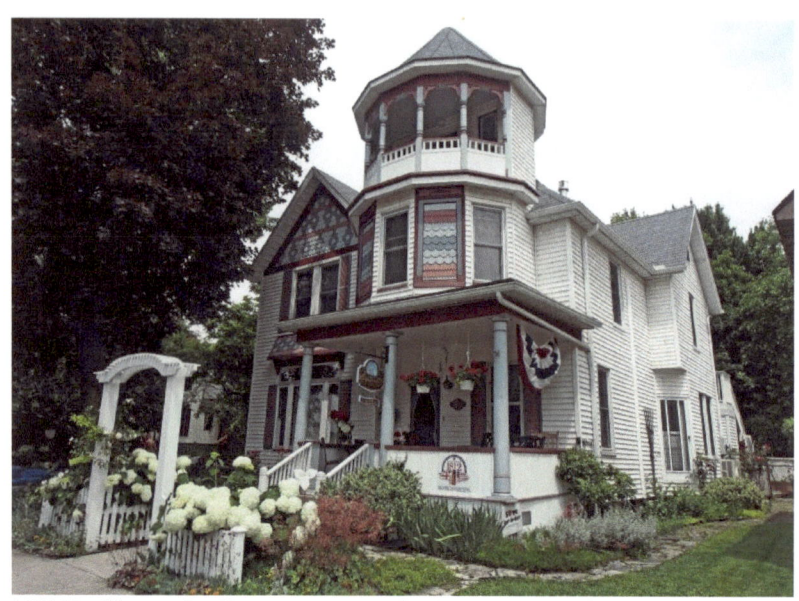

199 Dalhousie Street – Bondy House Bed and Breakfast Century old Victorian Queen Anne home, turret called "Widow's Walk" for a great view, trichromatic siding

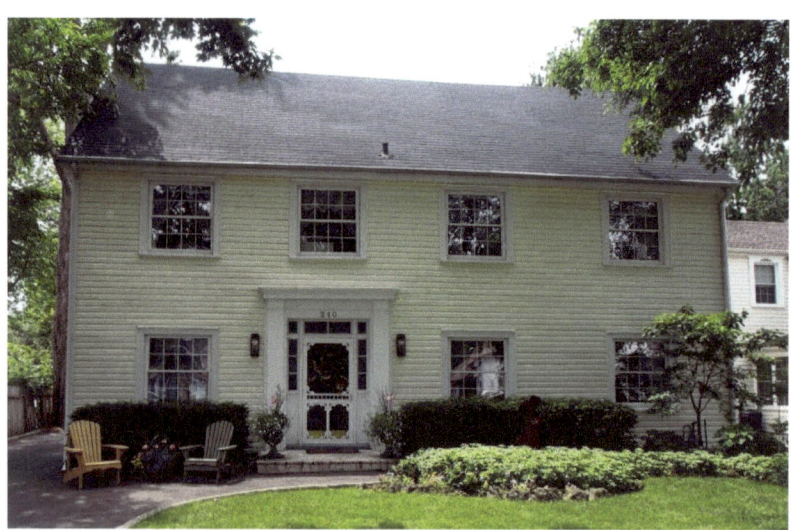

210 Dalhousie Street – Georgian style – board and batten, sidelights and transom window around door

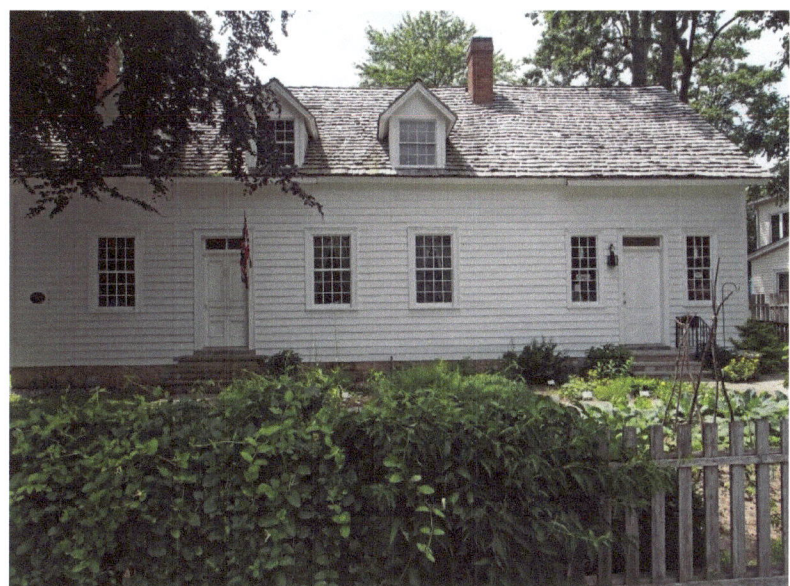

214 Dalhousie Street – Pensioner's cottage - the oldest house in Amherstburg (1796) – moved here from River Rouge, Detroit in 1798 by merchants Leith, Shepherd & Duff; purchased in 1838 by Thomas F. Park and owned by the Park Family (tinsmiths) until 1945 – moved to this site in 1972 and restored by the Rotary Club of Amherstburg as the Park House Museum - very early example of solid log, French frame construction; three dormers, Victorian style

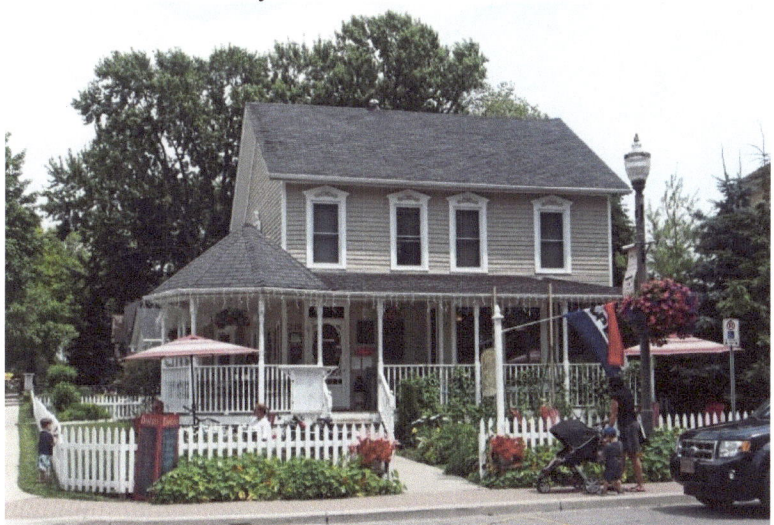

219 Dalhousie Street – decorative window hoods, cove siding, carpenters' Gothic window casings

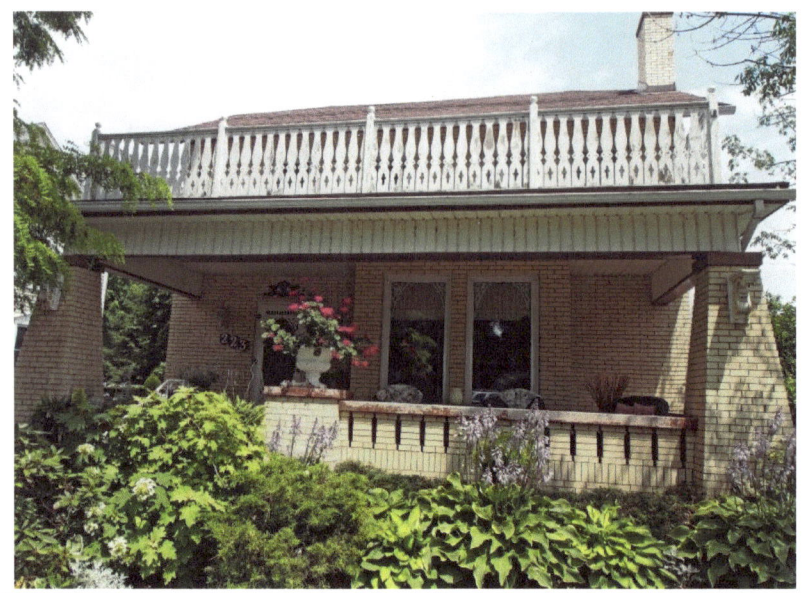

223 Dalhousie Street – second floor wraparound balcony

The Great Sauk Trail

The Great Sauk Trail, part of an ancient network of Indian paths, extended from Rock Island in Illinois to the Detroit River. It played a significant role in the communications between the native peoples in the upper Mississippi Valley and the British in this region particularly during the period of Anglo-American rivalry following the American Revolution. For four decades pro-British tribes such as the Sauk and the Fox made annual pilgrimages along the trail to Fort Malden where they met with officials of the British Indian Department and participated in gift-giving ceremonies reaffirming their alliance. When these exchanges were terminated in the late 1830s by the British, the Great Sauk Trail gradually fell into disuse.

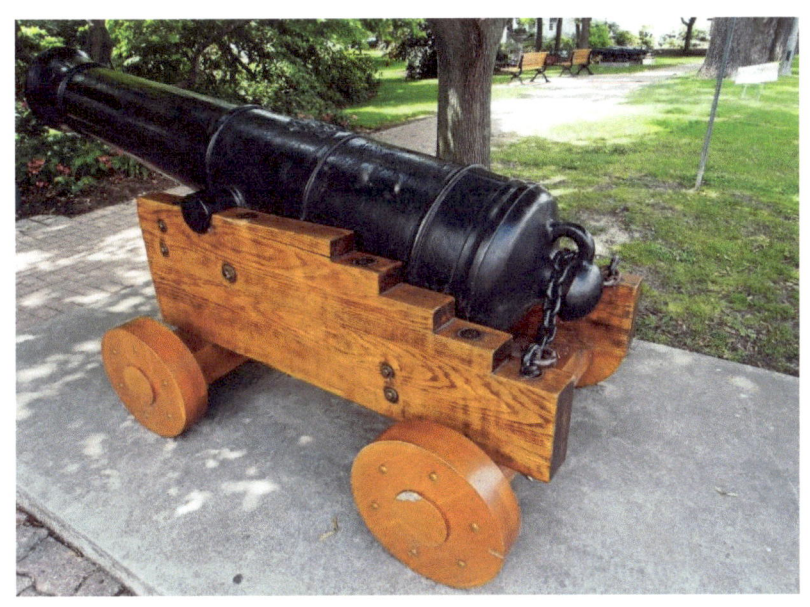

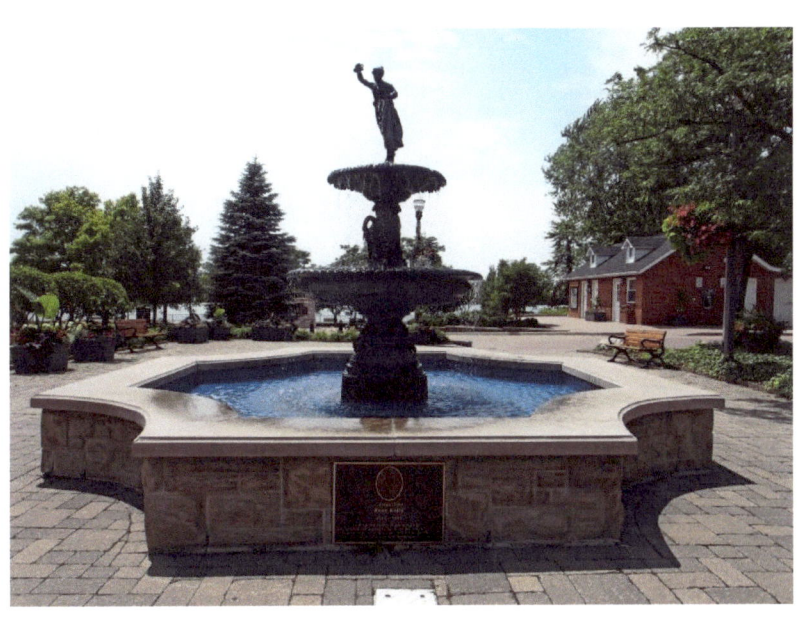

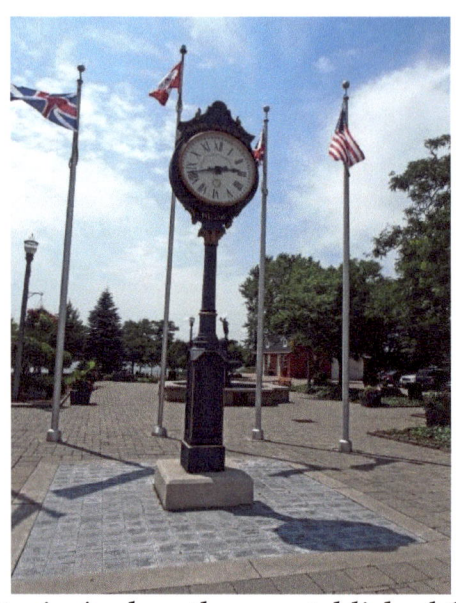

Historic Amherstburg established 1796

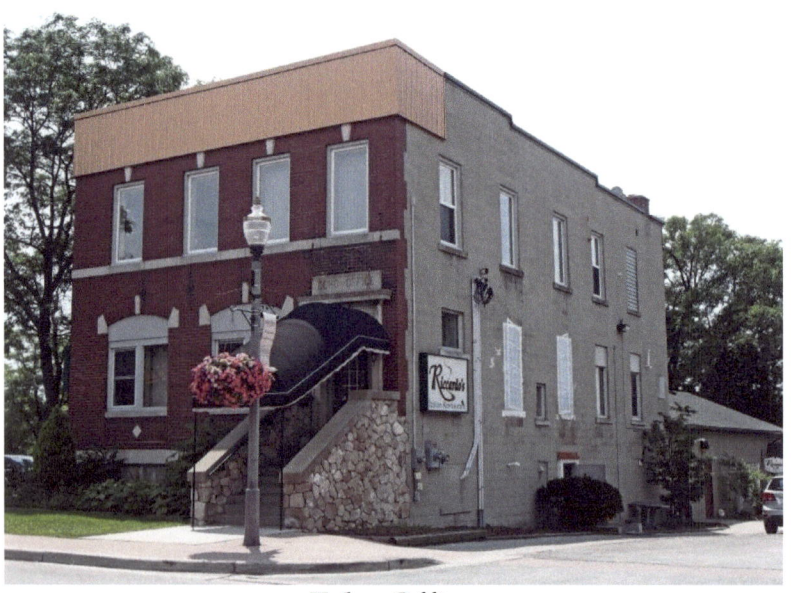

Echo Office

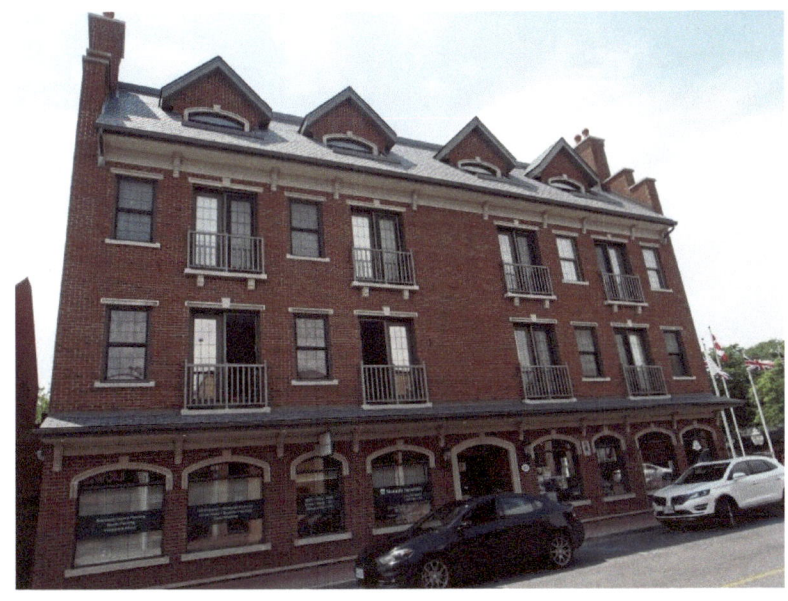

252 Dalhousie Street - former site of the Salmoni Building built
in 1849 which was demolished to create these condominiums
Cornice brackets, dormers

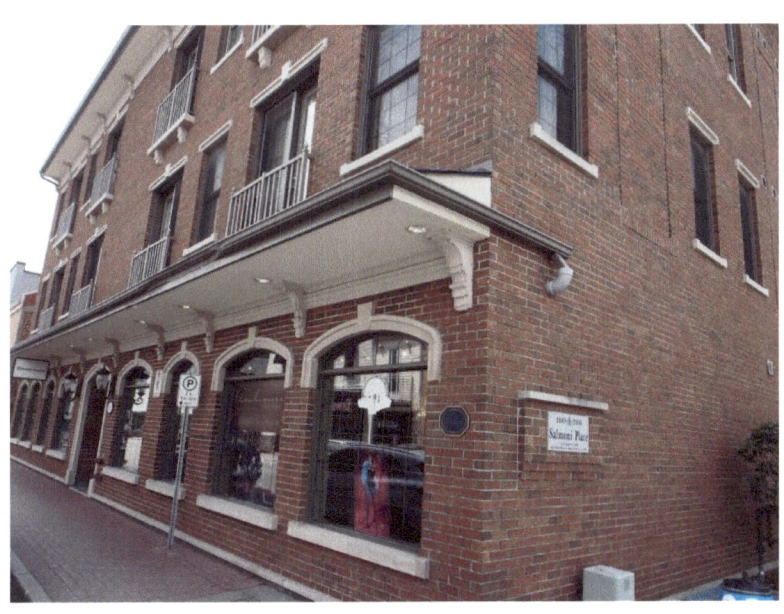

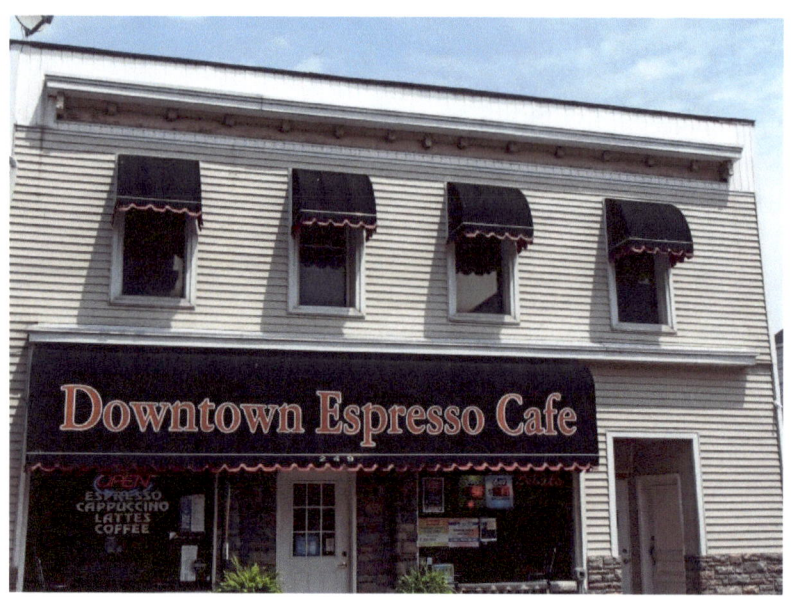

249 Dalhousie Street

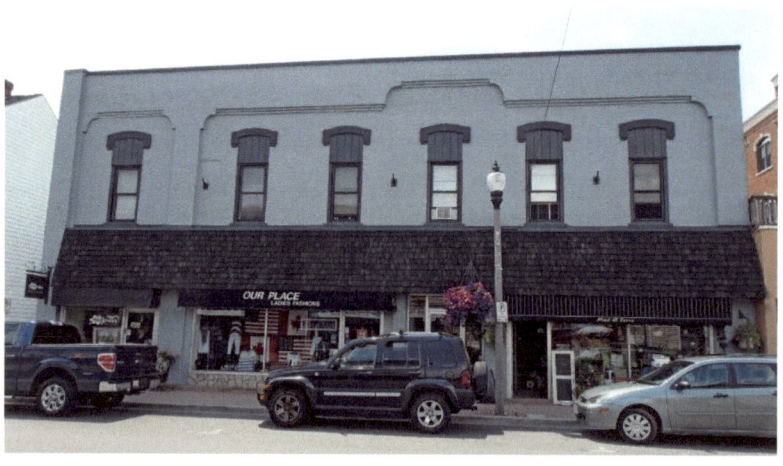

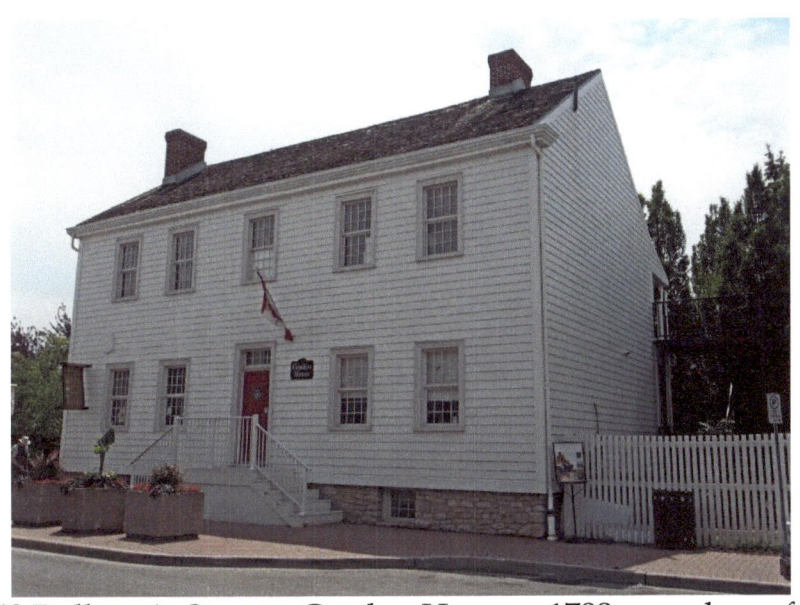

268 Dalhousie Street – Gordon House – 1798 – used as a fur trading post during the War of 1812
Board and batten – Georgian style

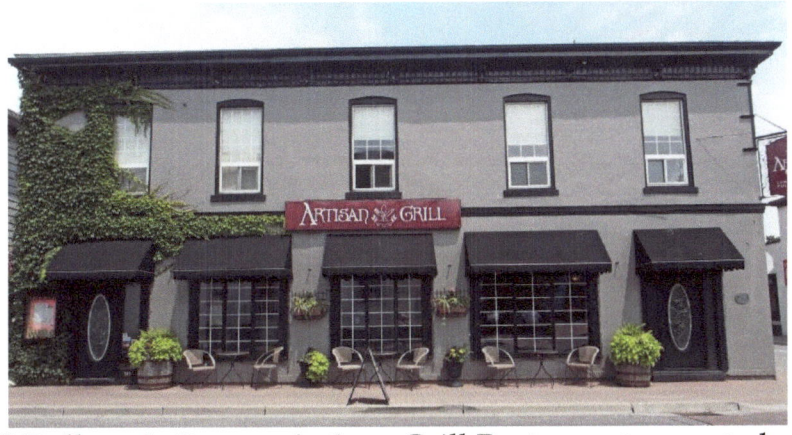

269 Dalhousie Street - Artisan Grill Restaurant – erected as a hotel and tavern in 1867

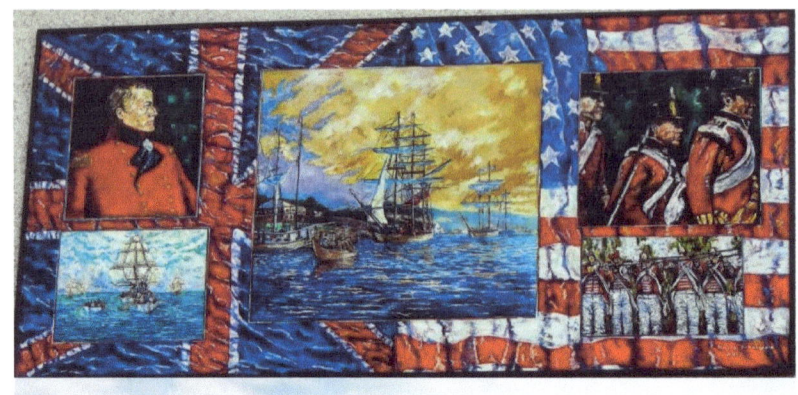

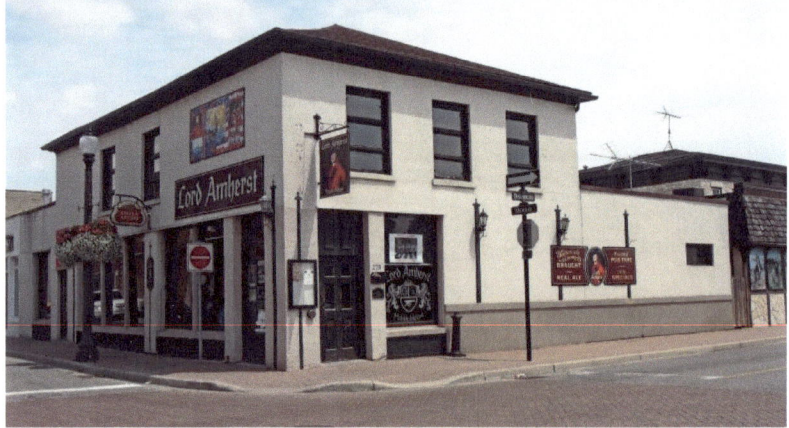

273 Dalhousie Street - Lord Amherst – Bullocks Tavern 1836
2-storey brick building, hipped roof

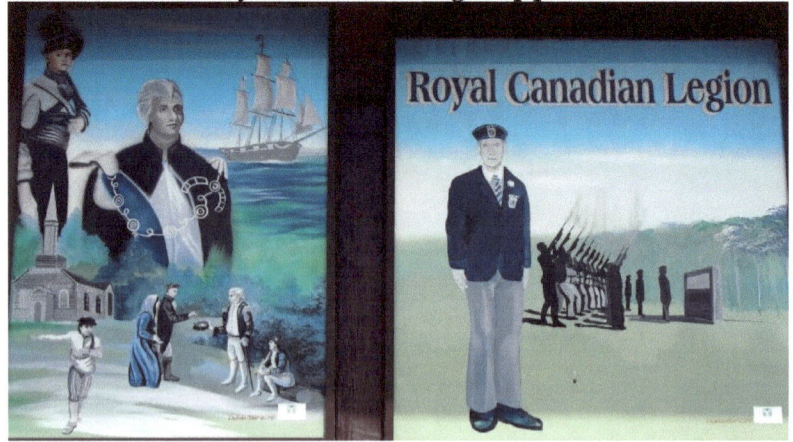

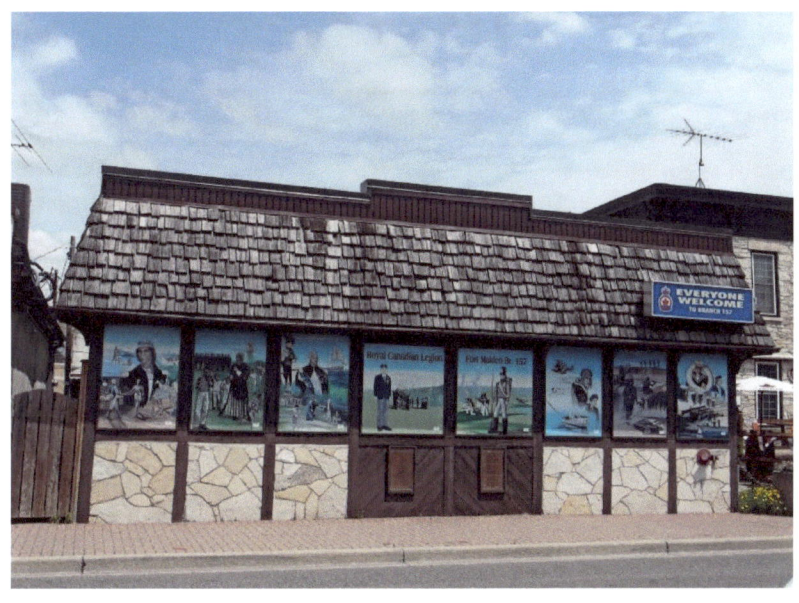

Dalhousie Street - Royal Canadian Legion

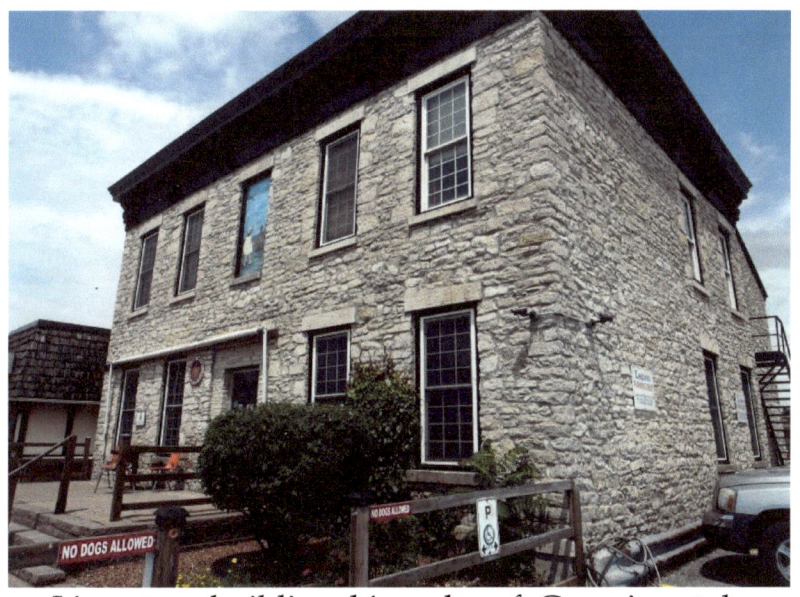

Limestone building, hipped roof, Georgian style

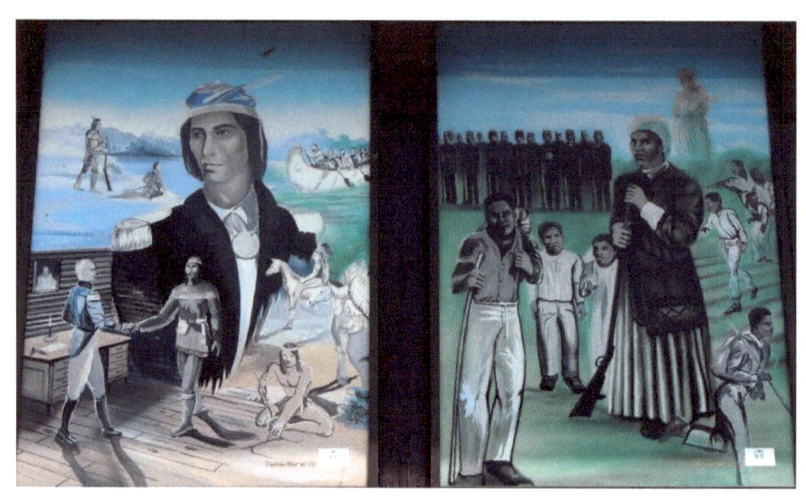

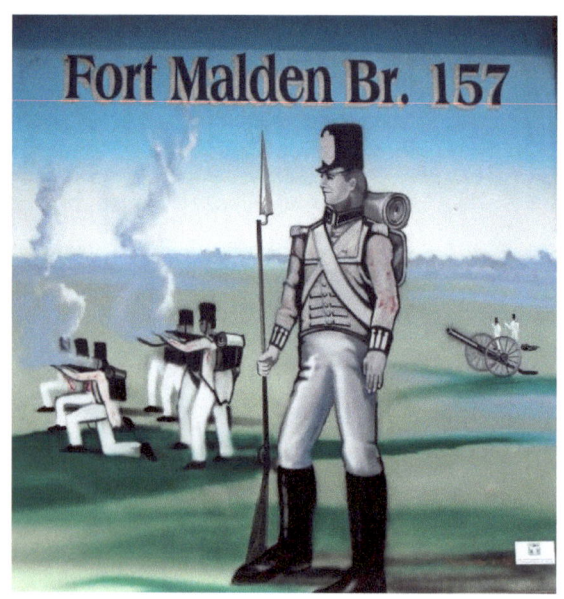

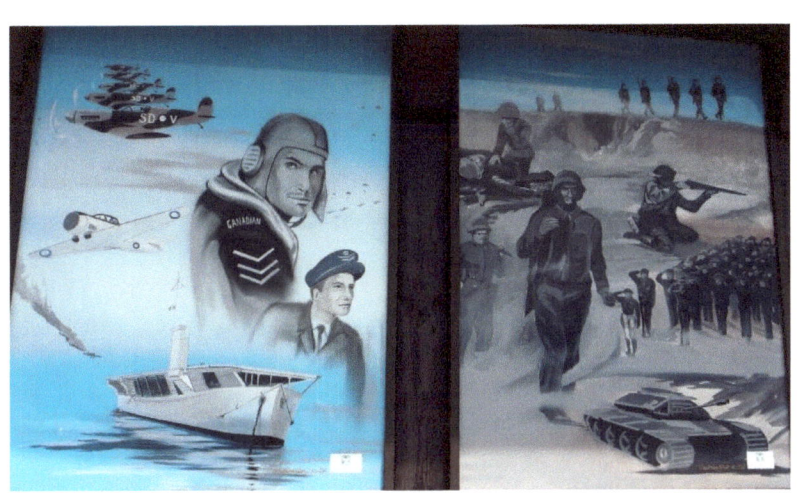
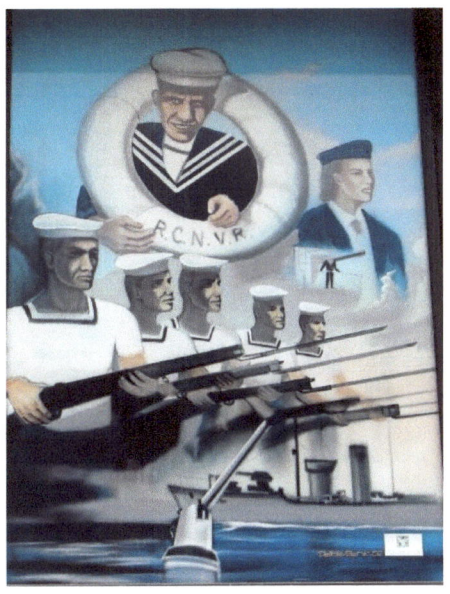

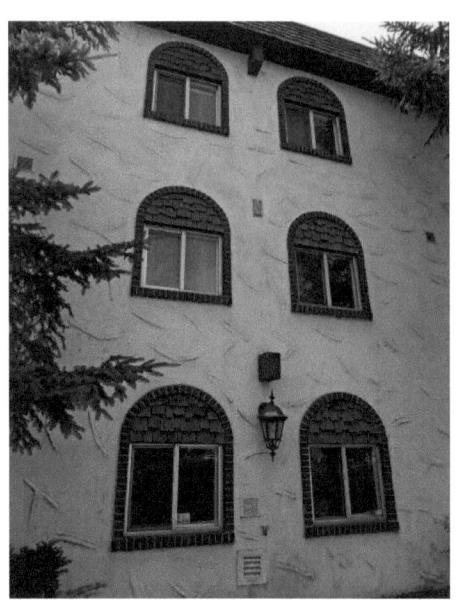

101 Dalhousie Street – textured plaster

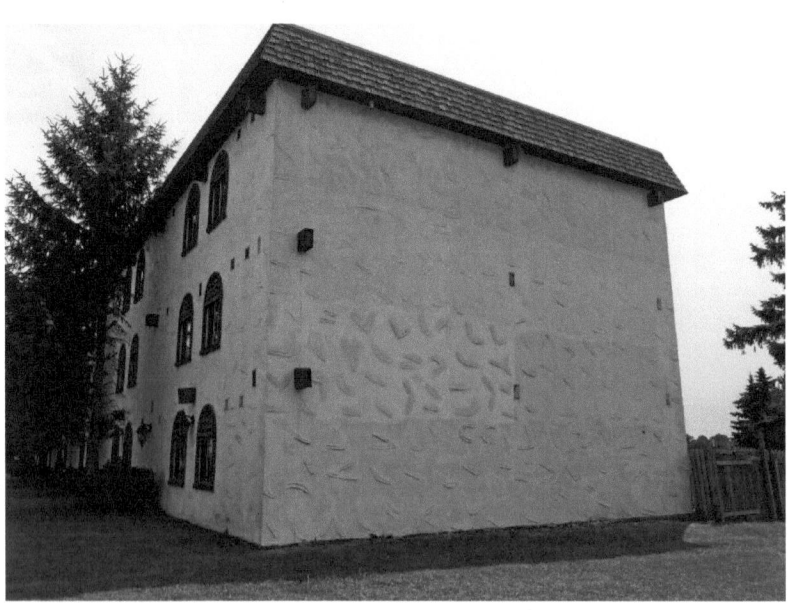

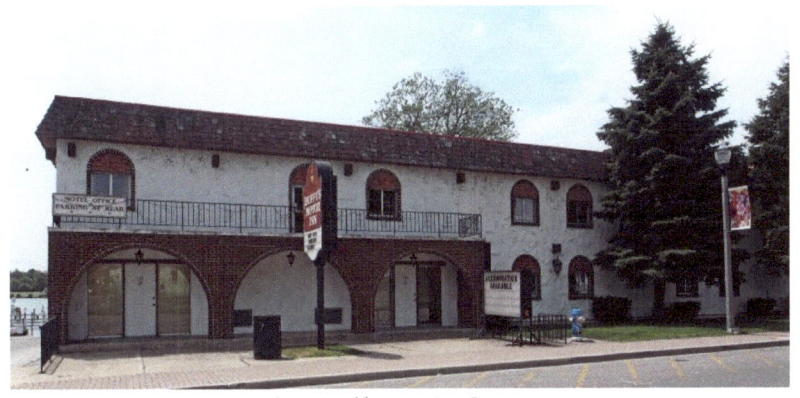

101 Dalhousie Street

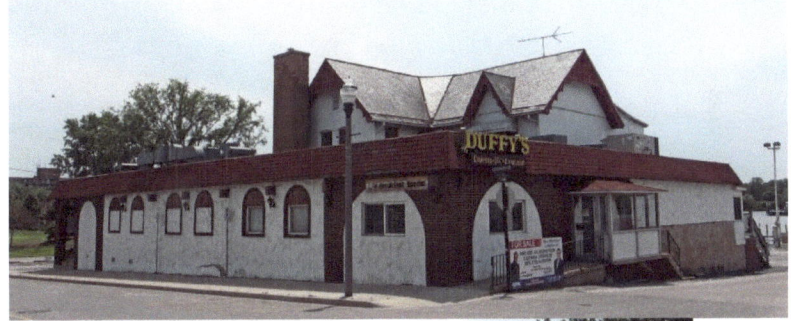

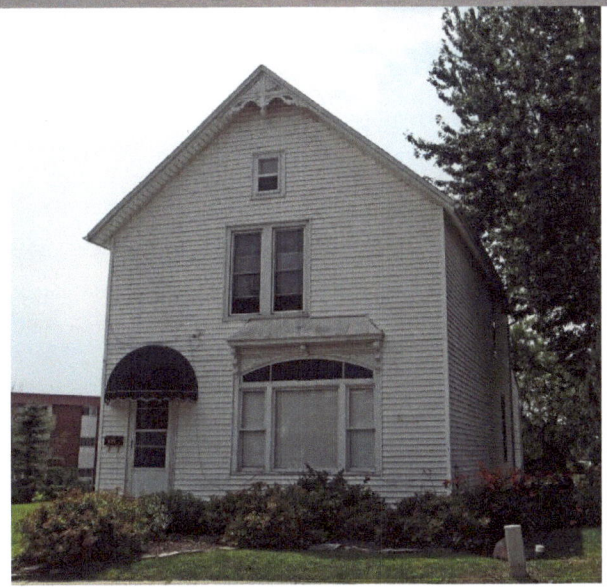

356 Dalhousie Street – Gothic – verge board trim,
Board and batten

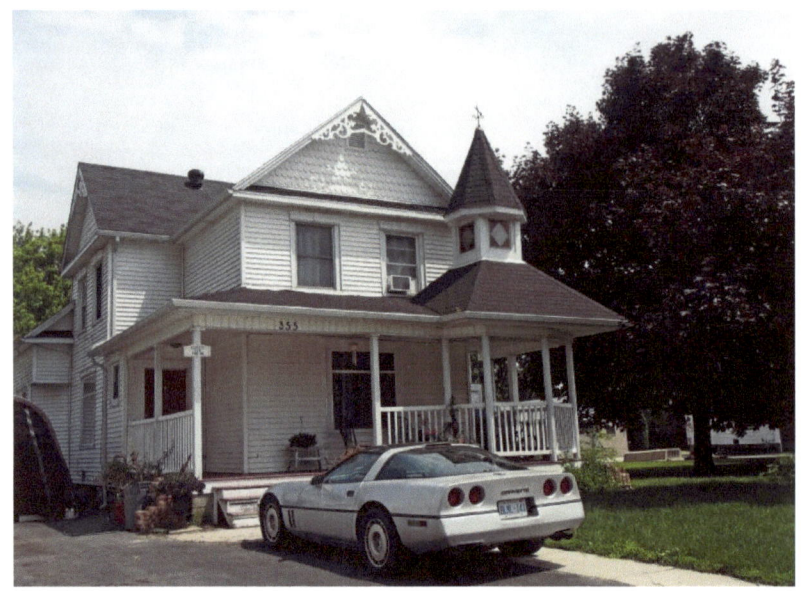

355 Dalhousie Street – Gothic, verge board trim on gable,
board and batten, cupola

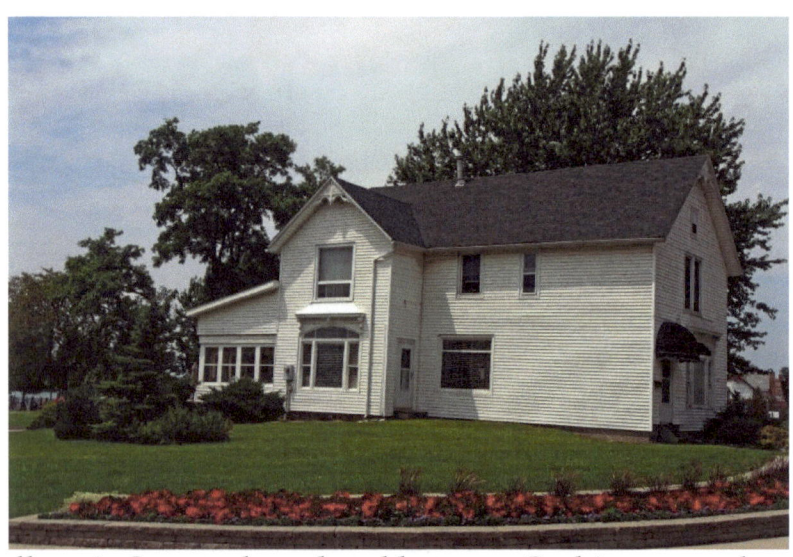

Dalhousie Street – board and batten – Gothic – verge board
trim on gable

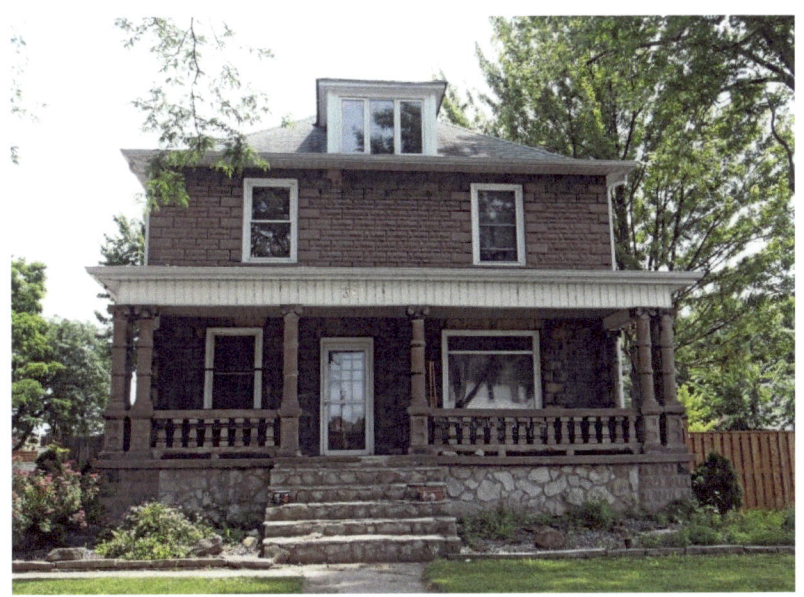

Dalhousie Street – cement block, dormer in attic

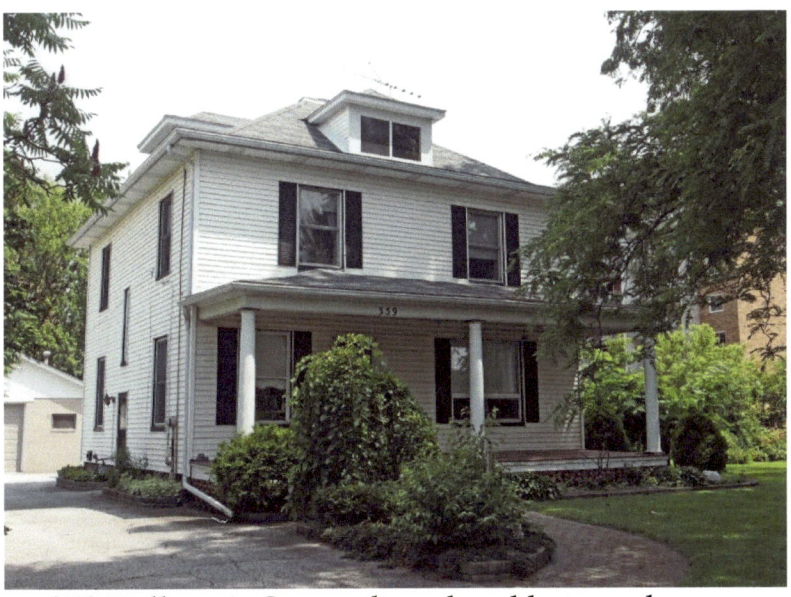

359 Dalhousie Street - board and batten, dormer

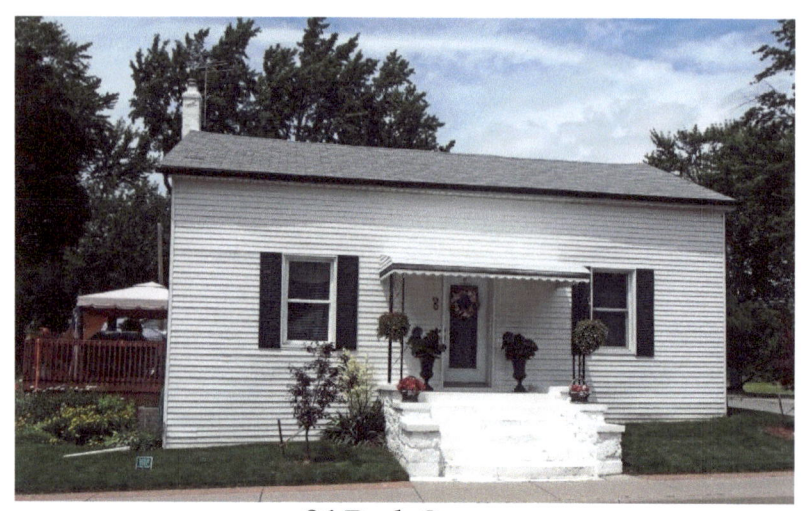

96 Park Street

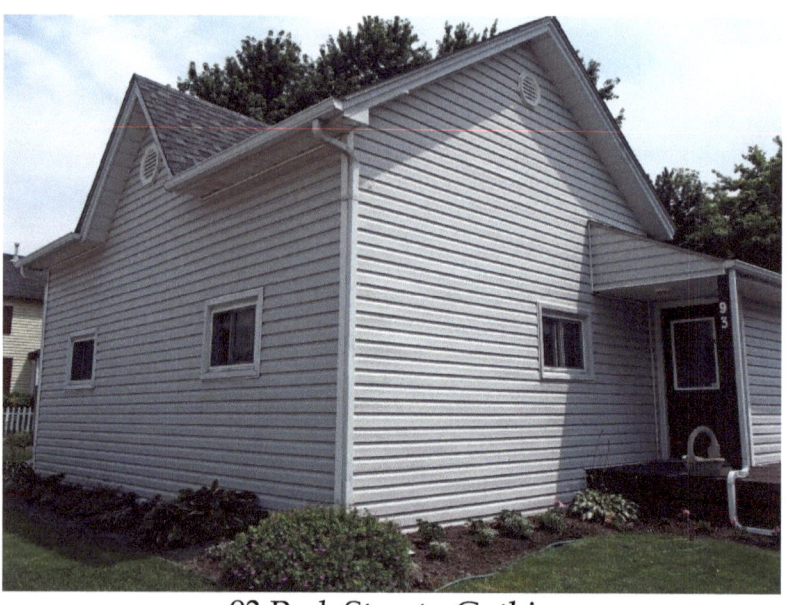

93 Park Street - Gothic

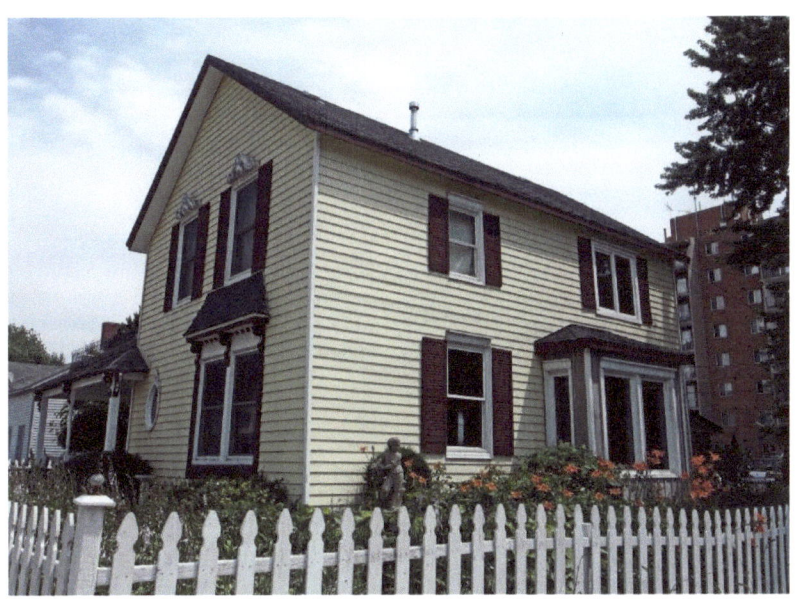

Park Street – Gothic, decorative window hoods, cornice
brackets, iron cresting around second floor balcony

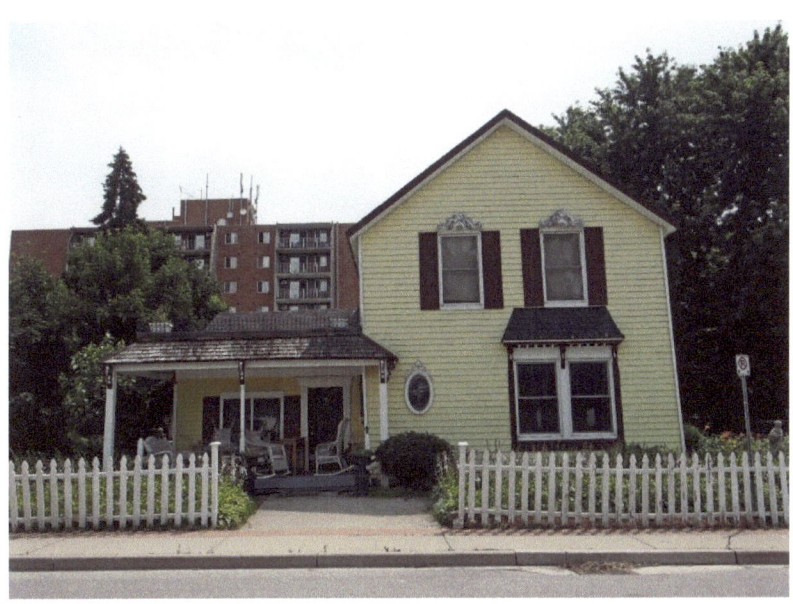

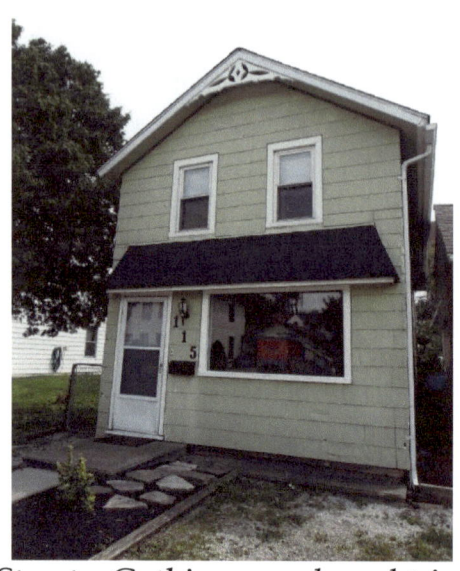

115 Park Street – Gothic, verge board trim on gable

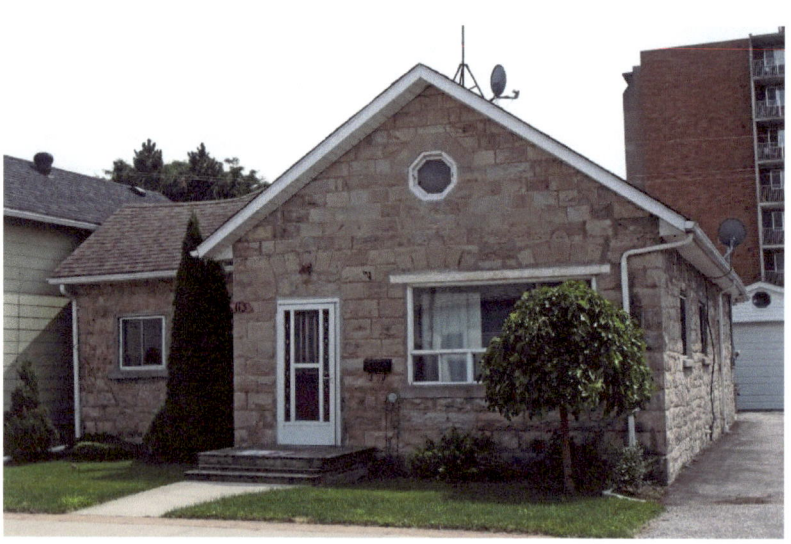

113 Park Street - stone

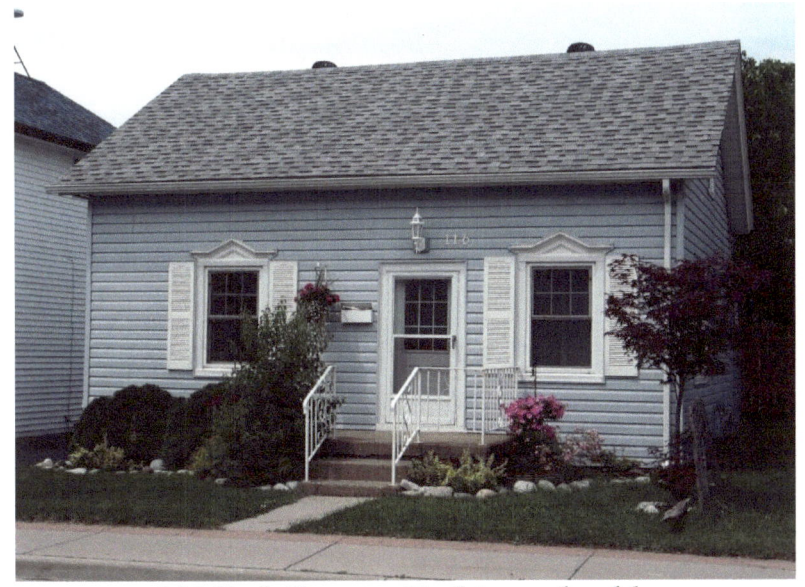

116 Park Street – Gothic, end gable

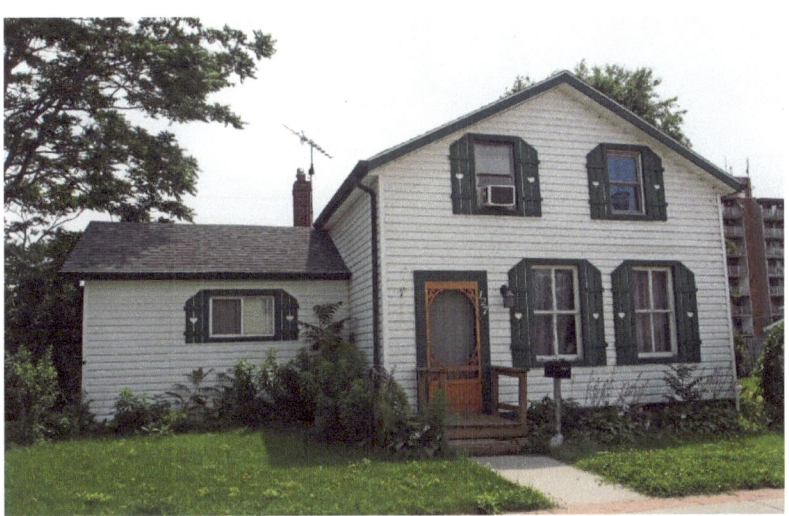

127 Park Street – Gothic, front gable, board and batten

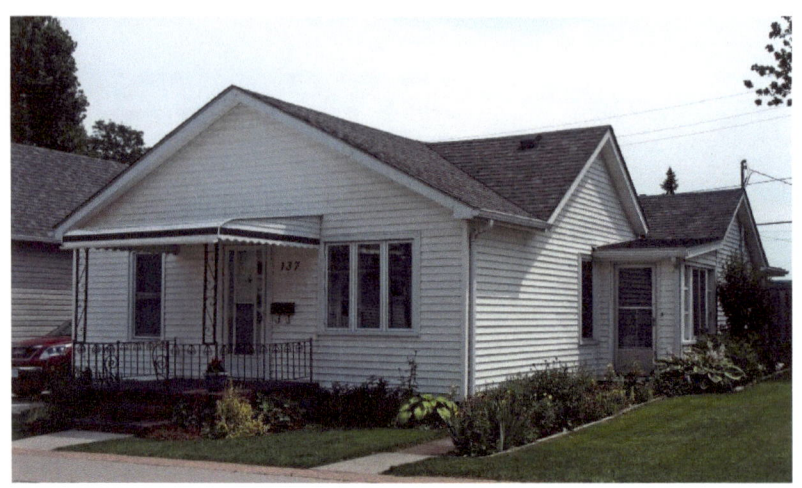

137 Park Street - Gothic

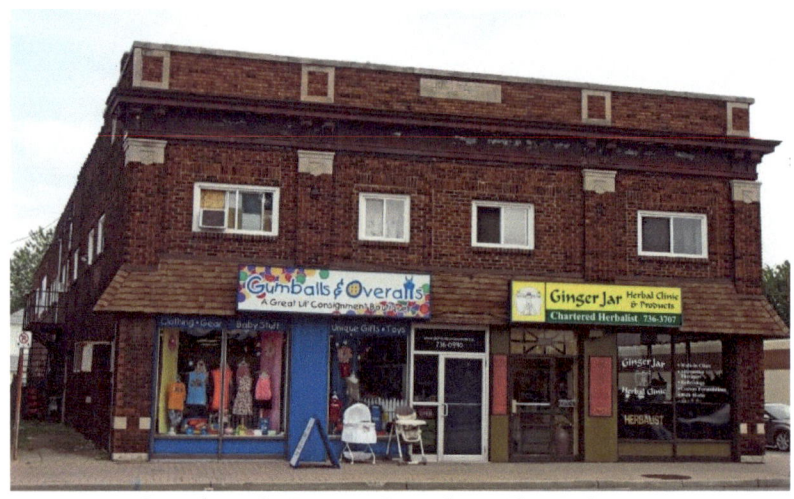

Sandwich Street South – The Liberty

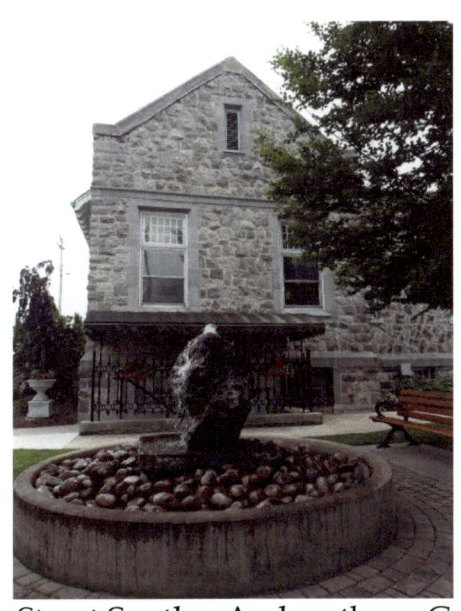

232 Sandwich Street South – Amherstburg Carnegie Public
Library – built in 1911 of limestone from the old Huron Indian
Quarry in Anderdon Township

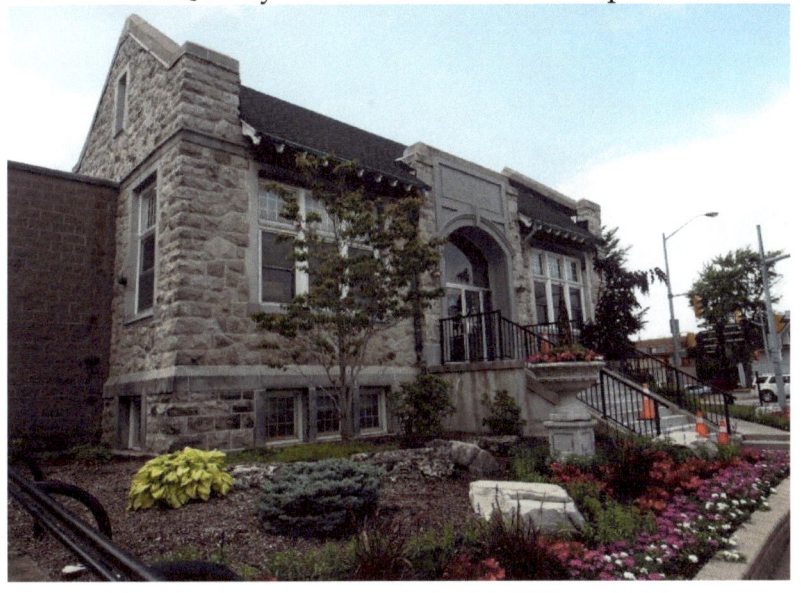

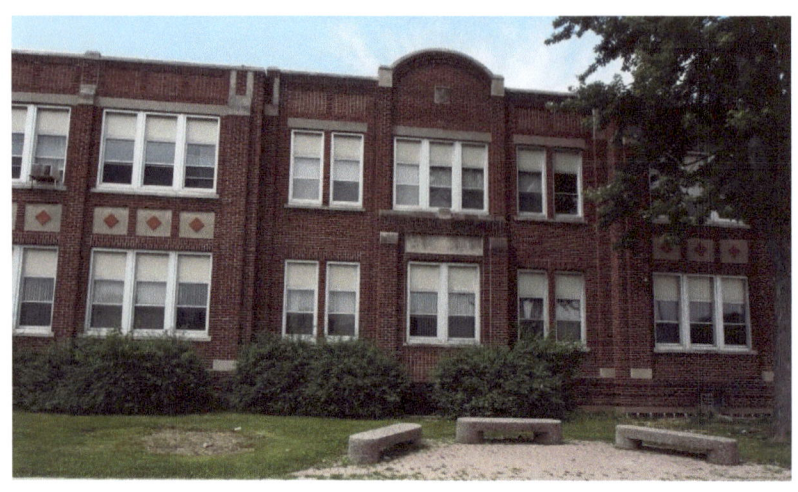

130 Sandwich Street South – General Amherst High School
Established 1914

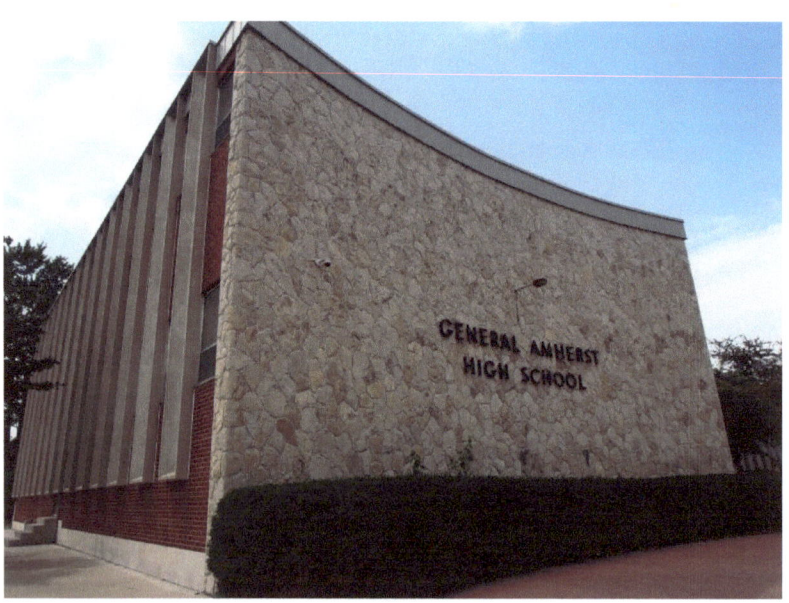

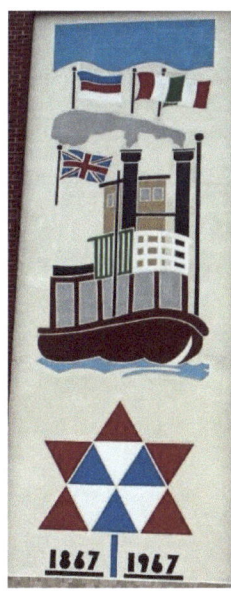

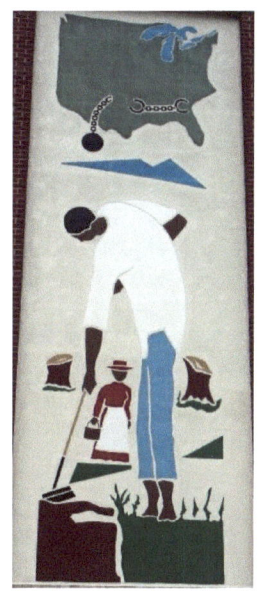

The year 1967 marked the year of Canada's 100th year of nationhood from coast to coast. Canada and Amherstburg's multicultural identity is expressed through the flags in the mural and the design of the official Canadian Centennial Logo.

North to Freedom

The roots of Black presence in Canada dates back to the early 17th century. Early Loyalist settlers in this area brought slaves with them. The Anti-Slave Law of 1793 forbade further importation of slaves into Upper Canada. The Abolition of Slavery Act ended slavery in Canada on August 1, 1834.

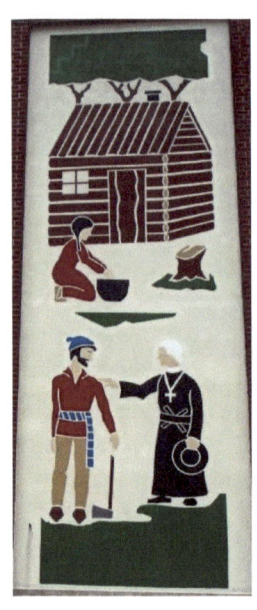

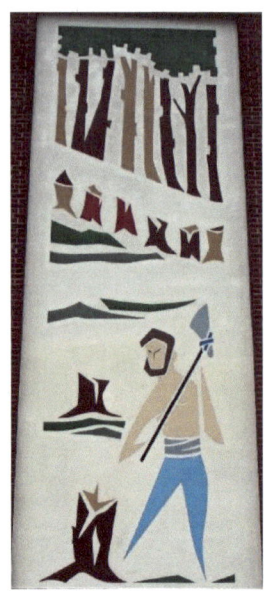

New France	**Agricultural Settlement**

In the late 1670s, French explorers and fur traders were the first Europeans to enter the lake region of Ontario. Missionary priests attempted to bring civilization to the frontier. In 1742 a mission house was established on Bois Blanc Island, the first place of Christian worship in Essex County.

Pioneer agricultural settlement in Upper Canada began following the American Revolution. Early settlers faced a land of Carolinian forest & swamp. Survival meant use of all available resources. A symbolic pioneer is portrayed amidst freshly chopped stumps with a forested background.

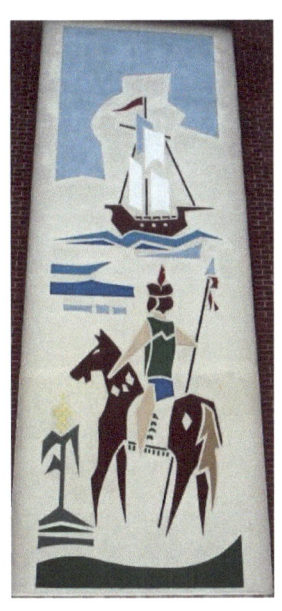

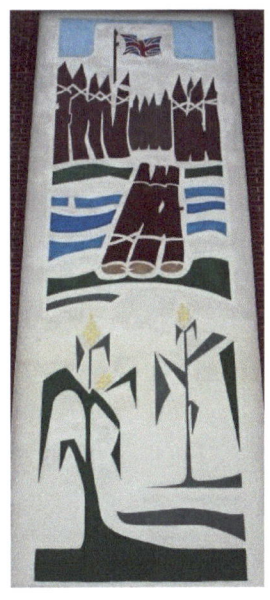

French Exploration and Aboriginal Contact

This mural represents the first European and First Nations cultural contact in this region. The contact and conflict of their cultures is portrayed strongly in this mural, a relationship which had a strong impact on the course of Canada's history.

Fort Malden 1796

Following the implementation of the Jay's Treaty on June 1, 1796 British military forces evacuated Detroit and relocated in Amherstburg (Malden). Corn is shown to indicate the growth of agriculture. The flag is the Grand Union, the flag of Great Britain before the union with Ireland in 1801.

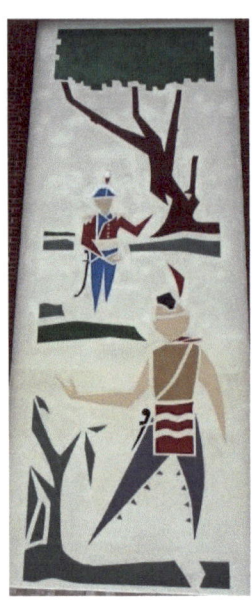

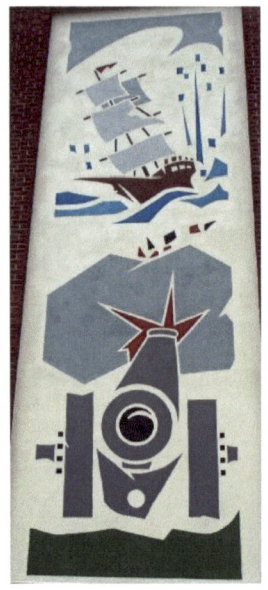

Tecumseh and Brock	Battle of Lake Erie September 10, 1813

This mural represents the Meeting of Chief Tecumseh and Major-General Isaac Brock. The First Nations allies under Tecumseh added essential strength to the British regulars and the Canadian militia to capture Detroit three days later without a single casualty.

This battle resulted in an American victory. The flagship of the British fleet's six vessels was the H.M.S. Detroit commanded by Commodore Robert Heriot Barclay. The United States nine vessel fleet was headed by the Lawrence and commanded by Commodore Oliver Hazard Perry. The strategic need to control the lake for military supply lines was paramount to both sides.

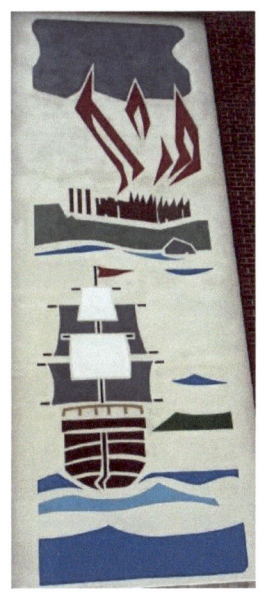 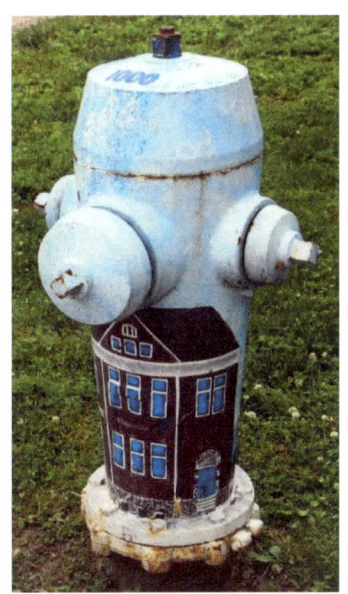

American occupation

This mural represents the American occupation of Amherstburg by American military forces following the Battle of Lake Erie in September 1813. Fort Malden was the only British fort in American hands at the date of the signing of the Treaty of Ghent on December 24, 1814. Fort Malden was returned to the British on July 1, 1815.

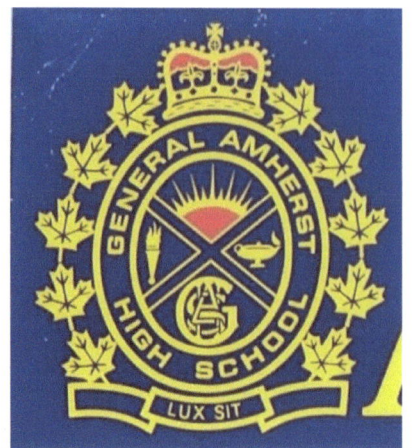

School crest

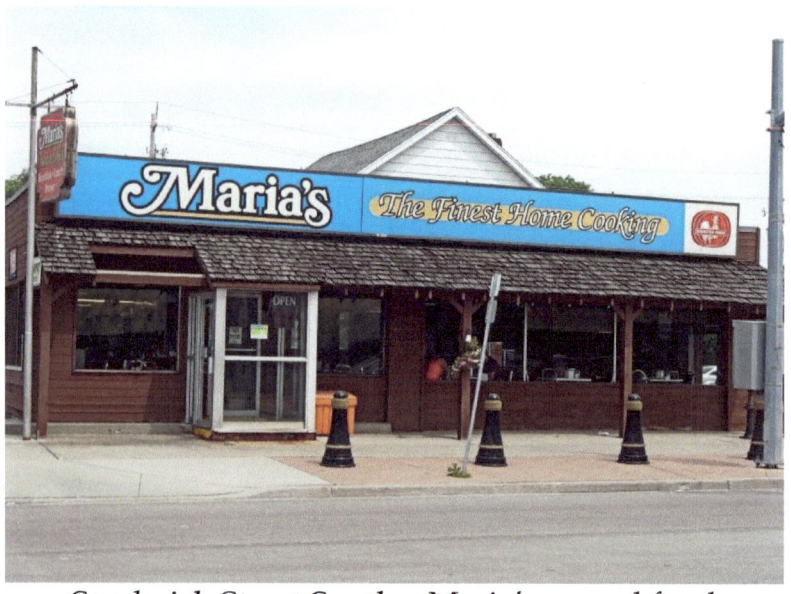

Sandwich Street South – Maria's – good food

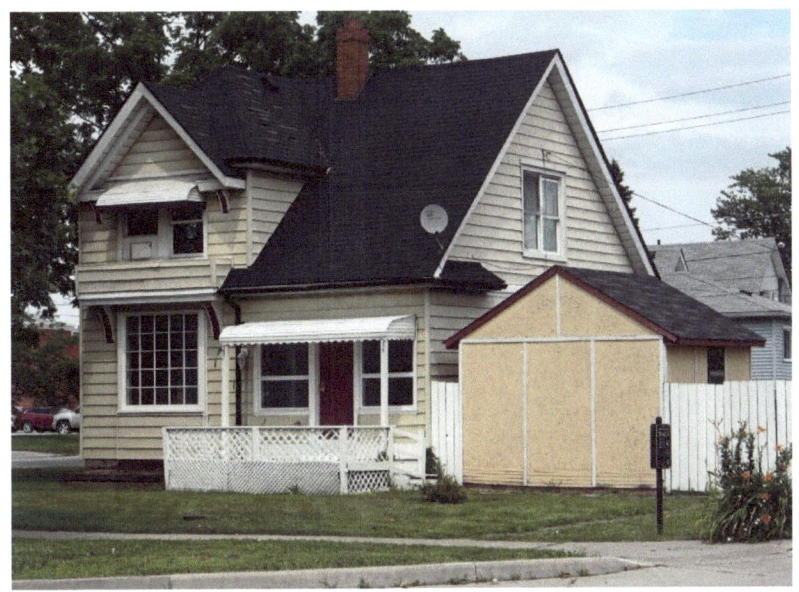

121 Sandwich Street South - vernacular

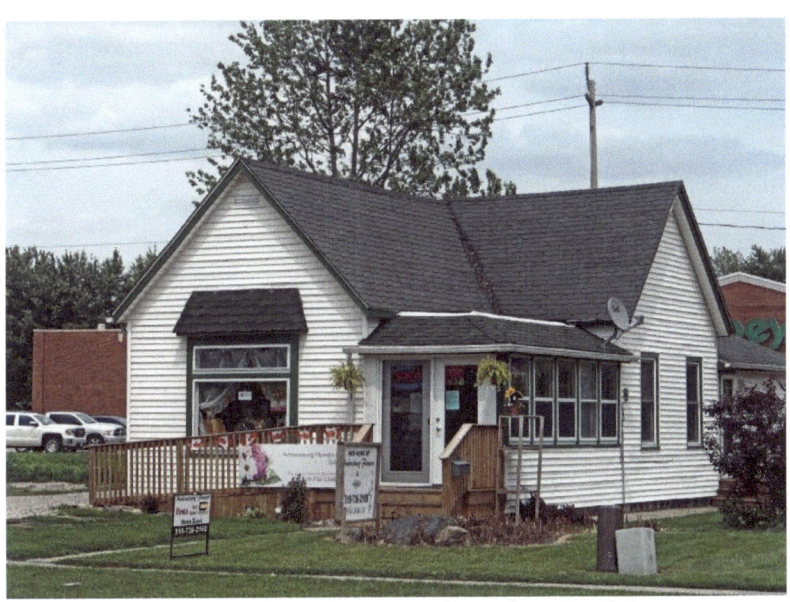

103 Sandwich Street South - Gothic

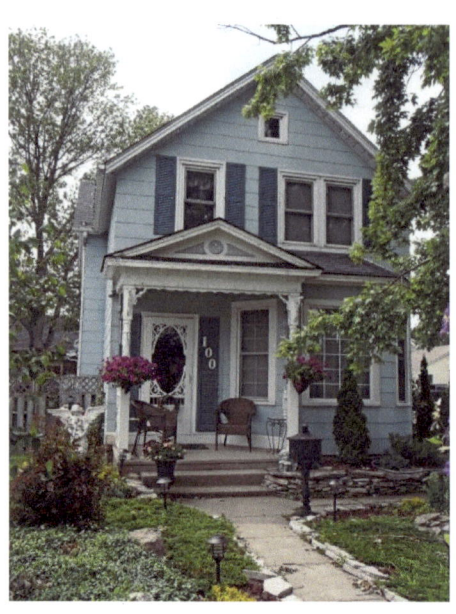

100 Sandwich Street South – Gothic – decorative brackets on porch supports, pediment

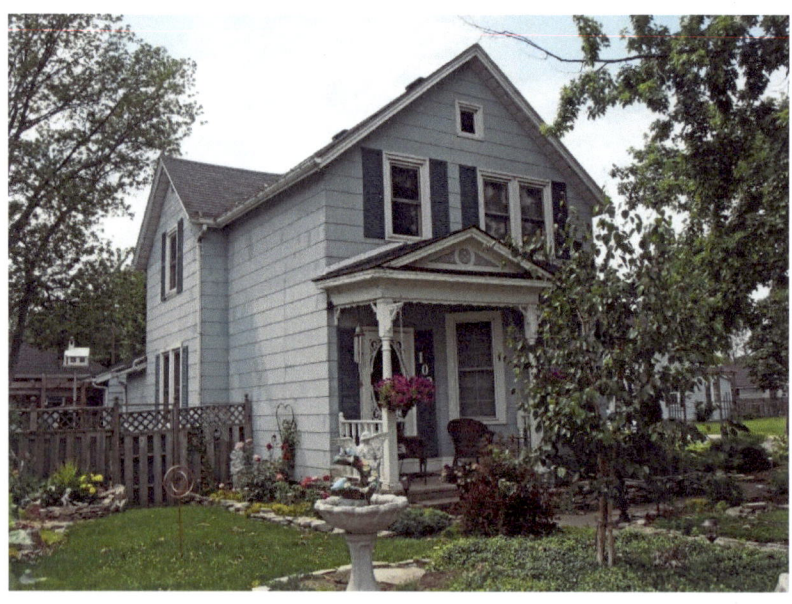

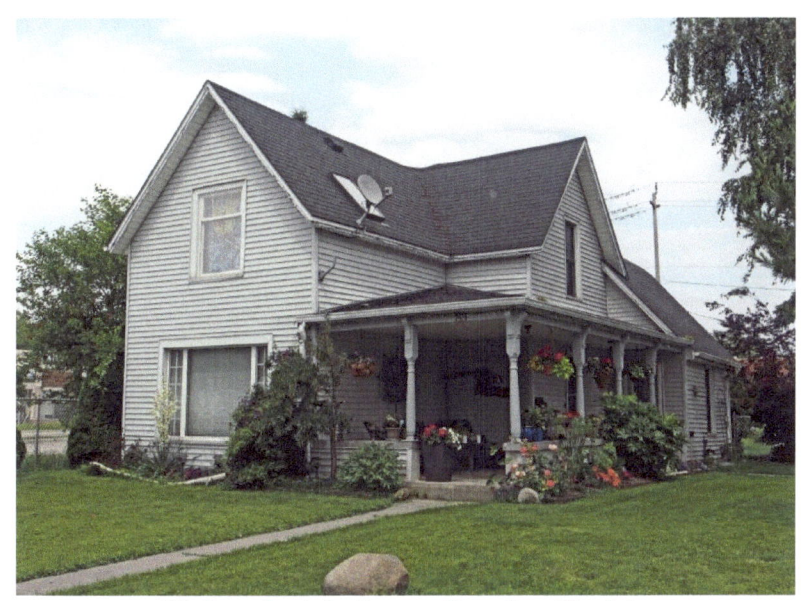

89 Sandwich Street South - Gothic

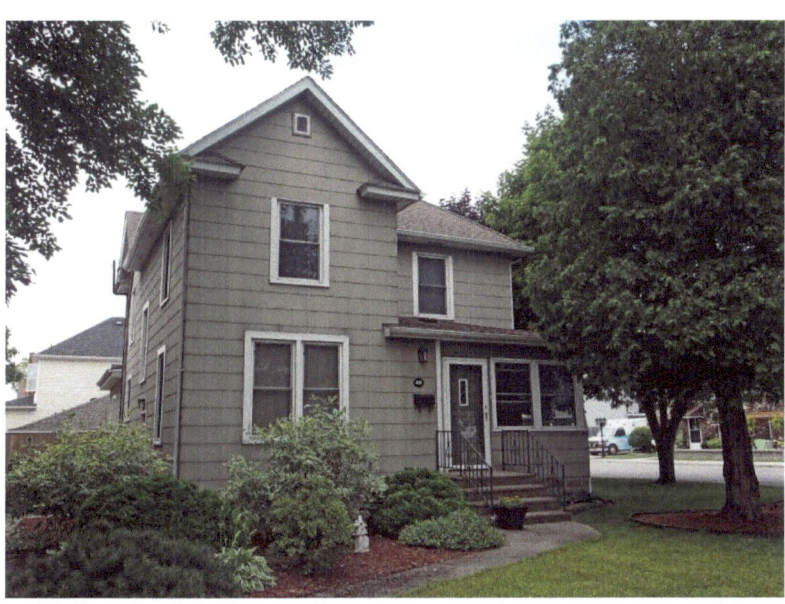

68 Sandwich Street South – cornice return on gable

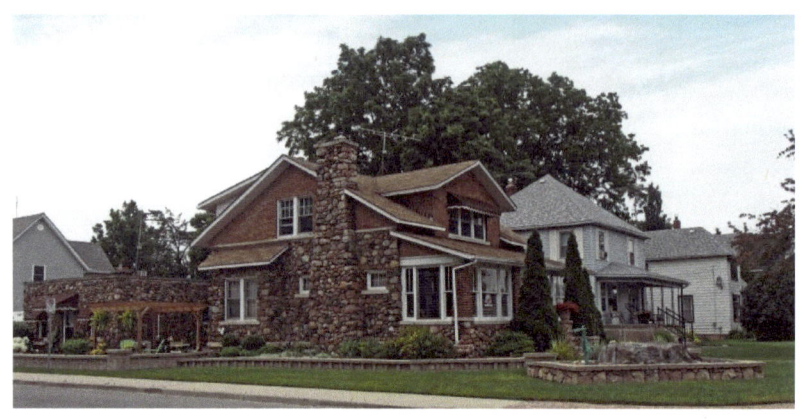

502 Sandwich Street South – Arts and Crafts style with cobblestones and brick - dormer

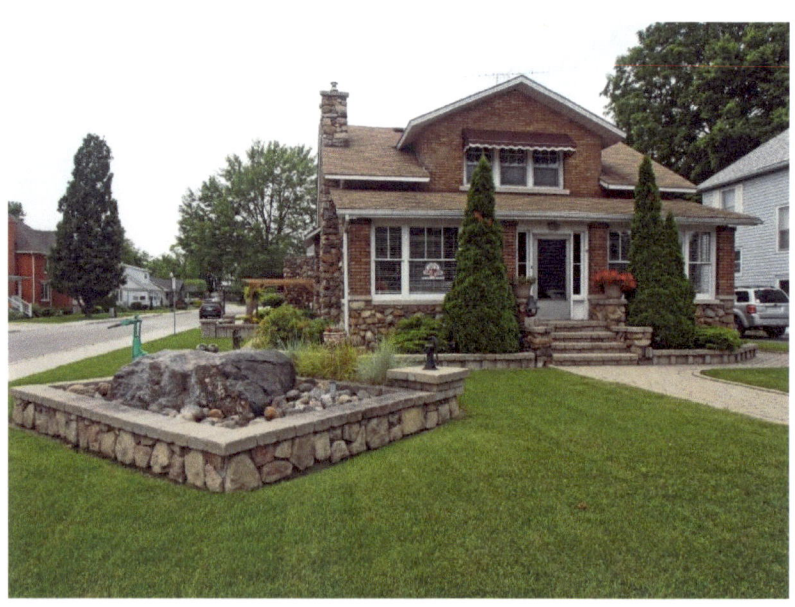

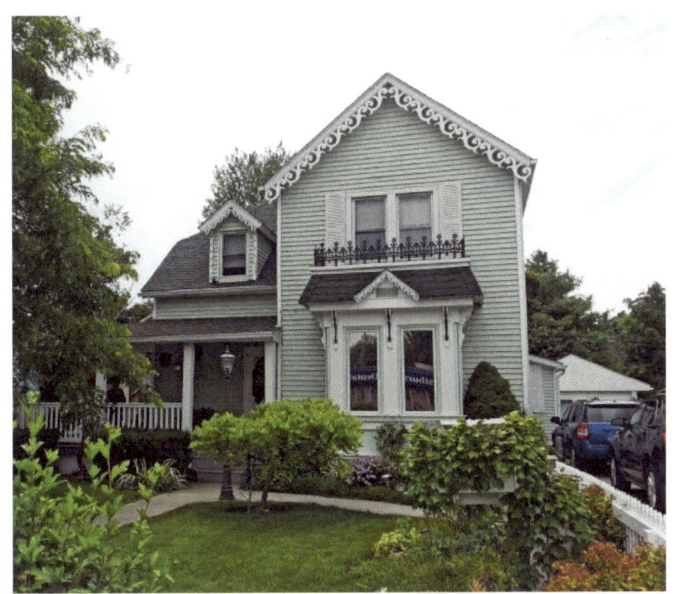

36 Sandwich Street South – Gothic Revival, verge board trim on gable, iron cresting above windows, cornice brackets, dormer above one storey section

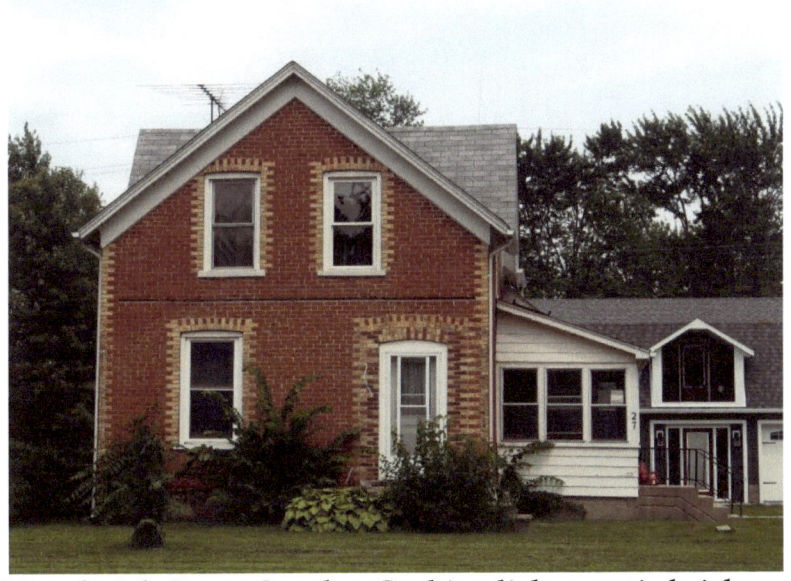

27 Sandwich Street South – Gothic, dichromatic brickwork

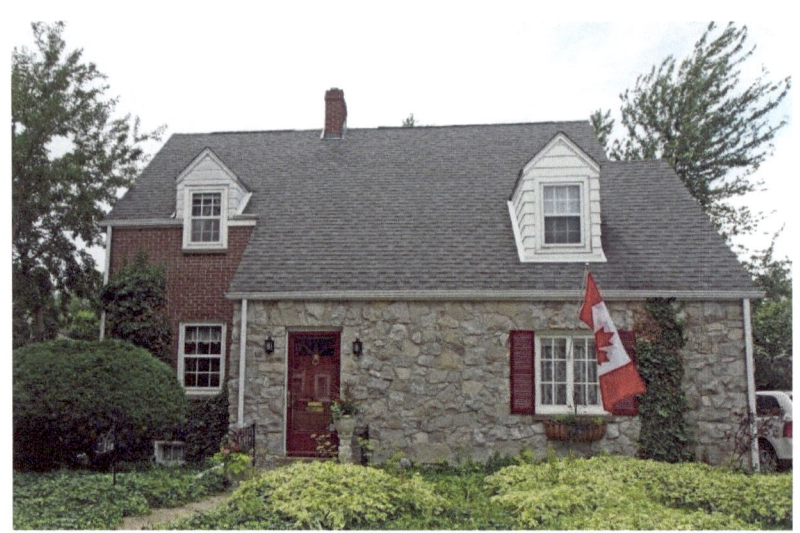

24 Sandwich Street South – dormers,
transom window above door

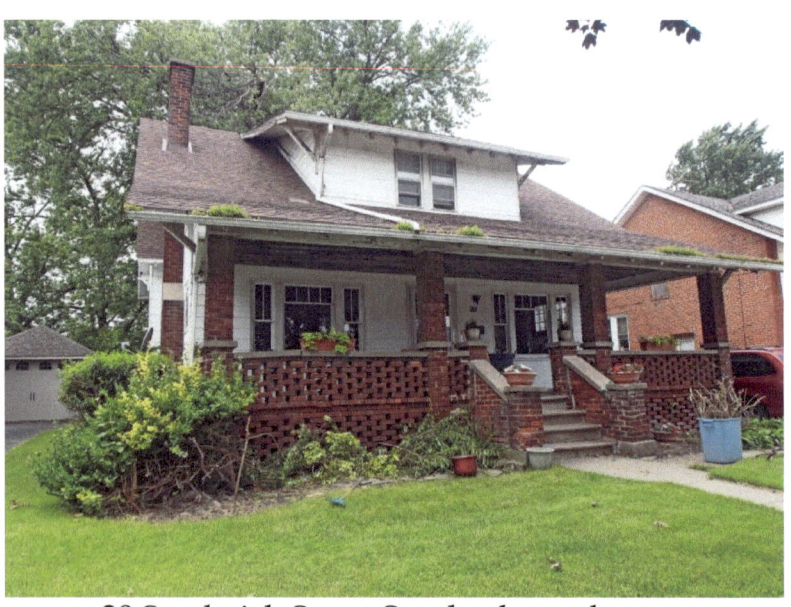

20 Sandwich Street South – large dormer

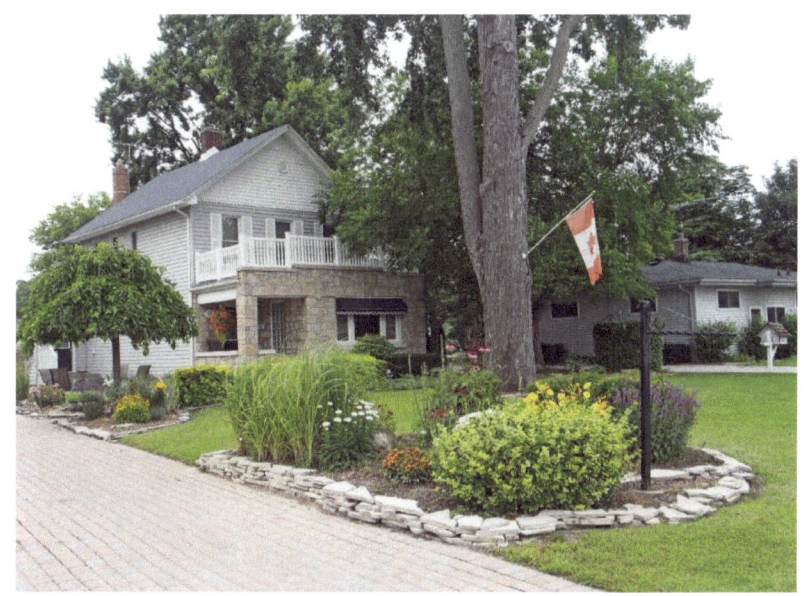

Sandwich Street South

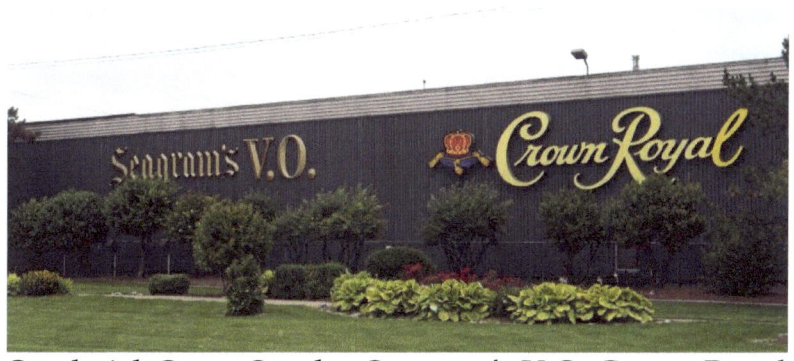

Sandwich Street South – Seagram's V.O. Crown Royal

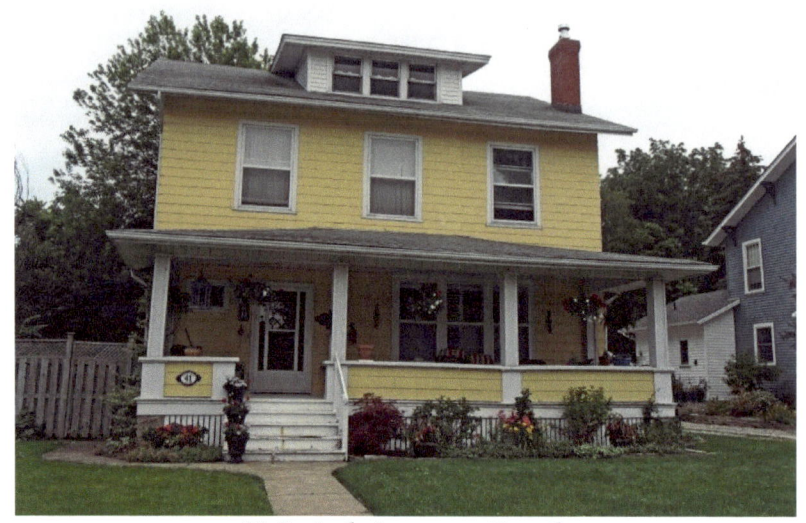

41 Laird Avenue South

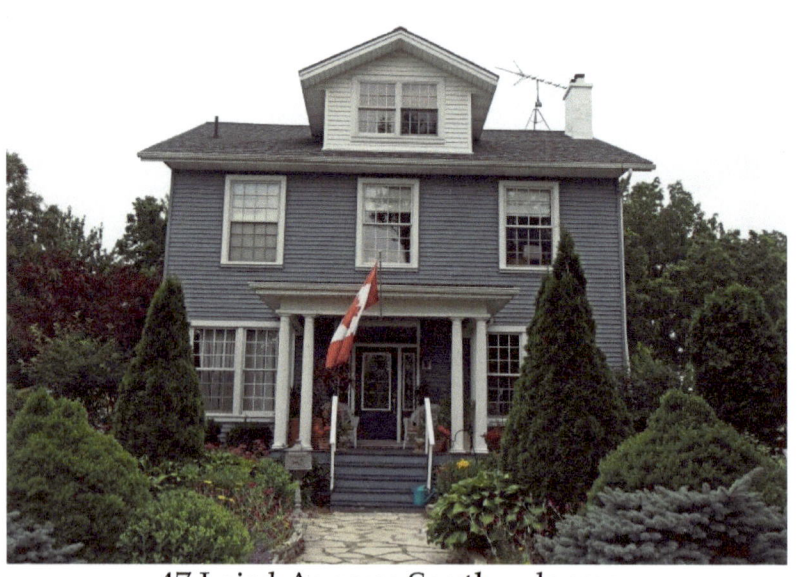

47 Laird Avenue South – dormer

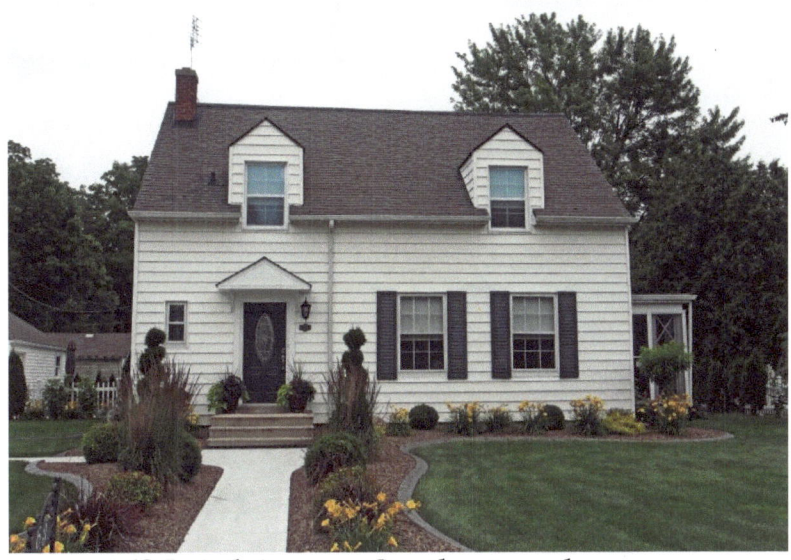

63 Laird Avenue South – two dormers

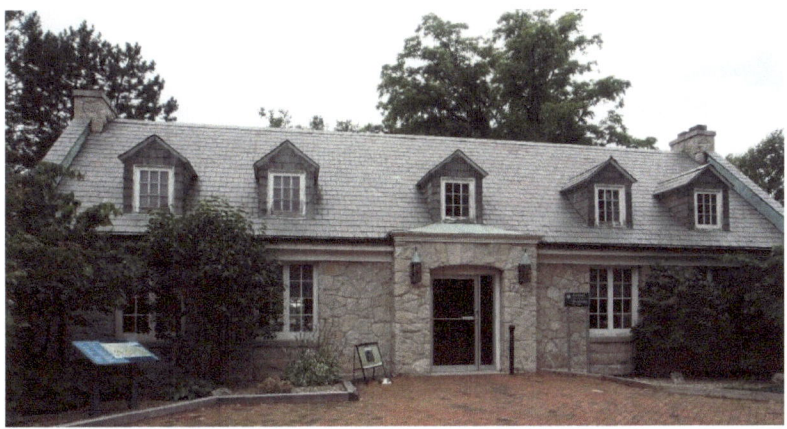

Fort Malden – This post was begun by the Royal Canadian Volunteers in 1796 to replace Detroit and to maintain British influence among the western Indians. As the principal defense of the Detroit frontier in 1812, it was here that Isaac Brock gathered his forces for the attack on Detroit. The next year, with supply lines cut, and control of Lake Erie lost to the Americans, the British could not hold the fort, so they evacuated and burned it. Partially rebuilt by the invading

Americans, it was returned on July 1, 1815 to the British who maintained a frontier garrison here until 1851.

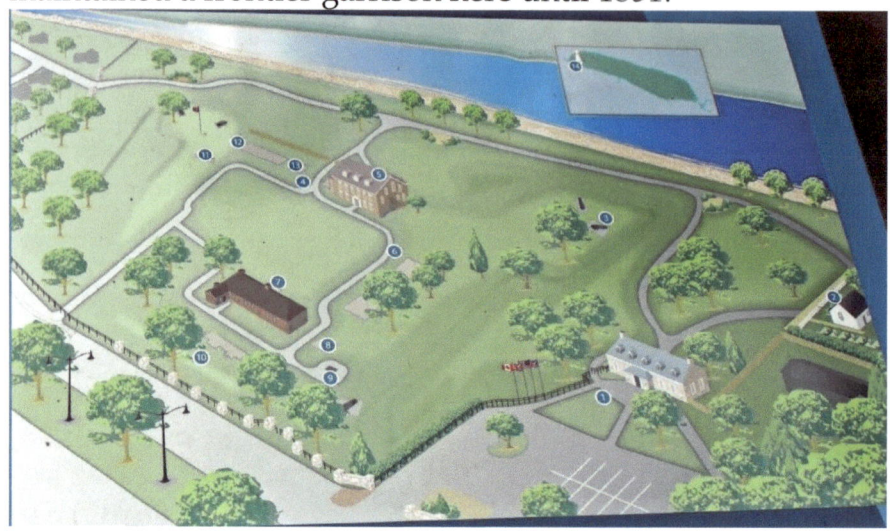

1 Visitor Centre
Military Pensioner's Cottage 2
5 Museum
7 Brick Barrack
Inset: Bois Blanc Island Lighthouse

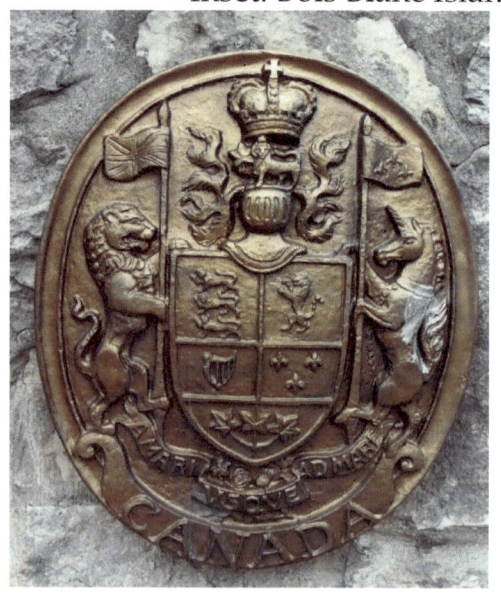

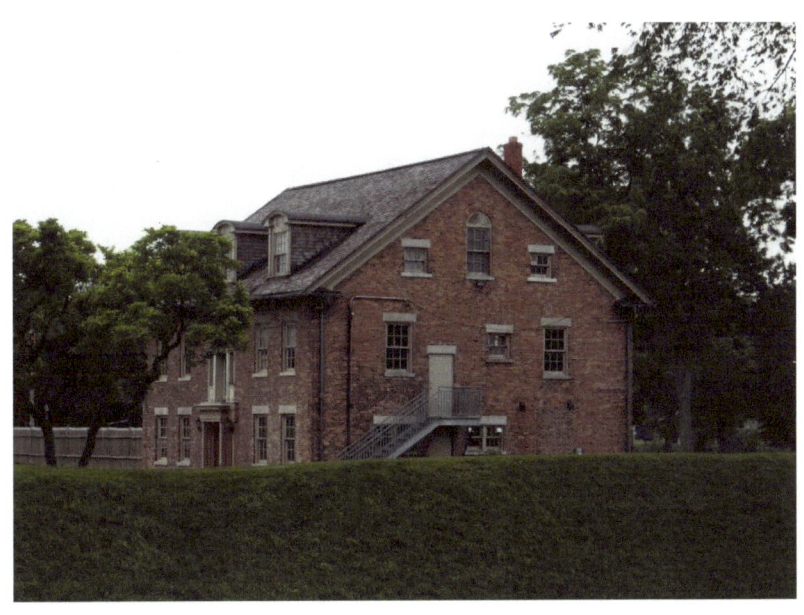

Fort Malden

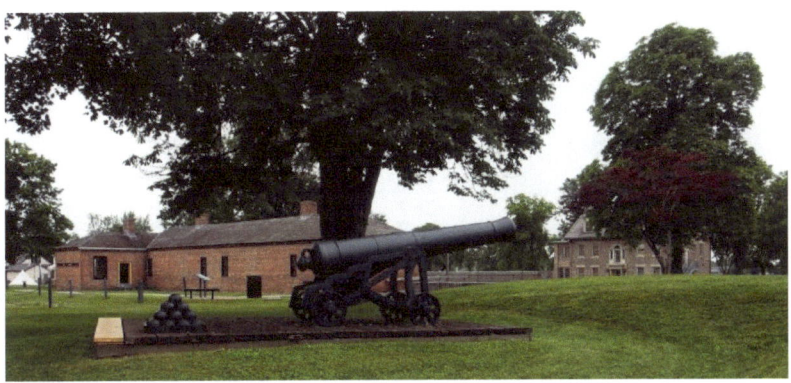

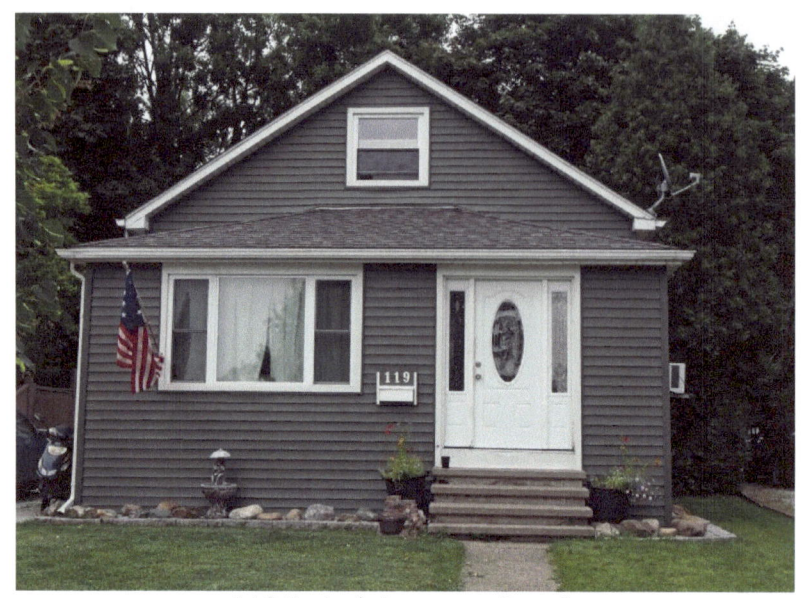

119 Laird Avenue South

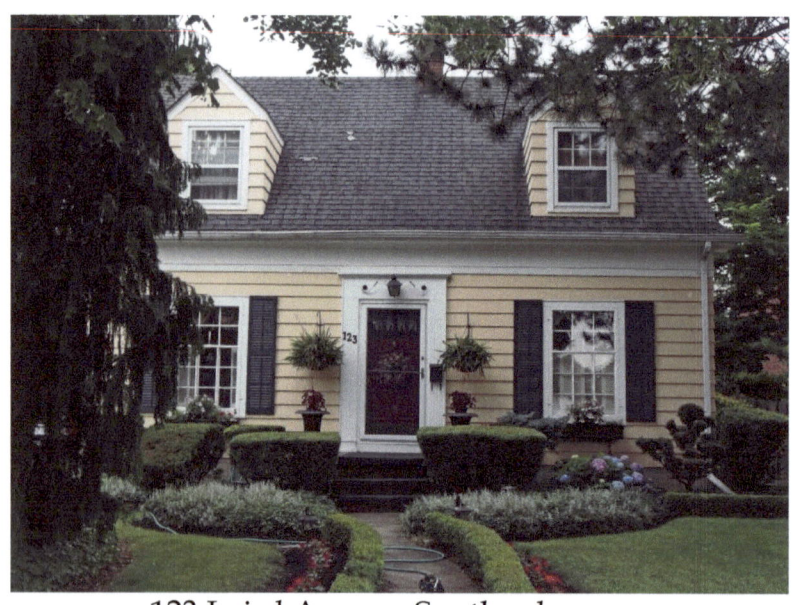

123 Laird Avenue South - dormers

Architectural Terms

Brackets: a decorative or weight-bearing structural element which forms a right angle with one side against a wall and the other under a projecting surface such as an eave or roof. Example: Dalhousie Street, see Page 8	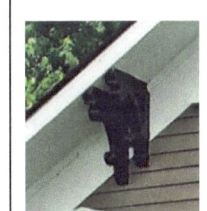
Capital: The uppermost finish or decoration on a column. An Ionic column has a small base, a thin elegant shaft, and a capital composed of volutes which are carved whirls or twists that take the form of a scroll. Example: 525 Dalhousie Street - Bellevue House	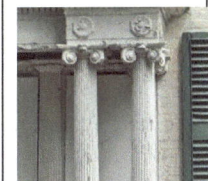
Cobblestone architecture: Refers to the use of cobblestones embedded in mortar as a method for erecting walls on houses and commercial buildings. Example: 502 Sandwich Street South	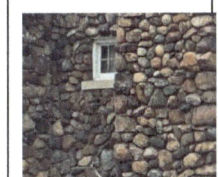
Cornice: originally the wooden overhang of the roof. With the use of stone, brick, iron and steel, the cornice is any projecting shelf at the top of a ceiling or roof. They can be very decorative. Example: 525 Dalhousie Street, see Page 11	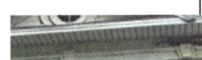
Cornice Return: decorative element on the end of a gable. Example: 68 Sandwich Street South	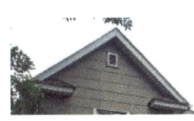

Cupola: A domed or curved roof rising from a building as a decorative element. Example: 355 Dalhousie Street	
Dentil Moulding: an even series of rectangles used as ornamental decoration in cornices. Example:	
Dichromatic brickwork: the use of two colours of brick, tile or slate to decorate a façade. Example: 27 Sandwich Street South, Page 49	
Dormer: (French for "sleep") a gable end window that pierces through the plane of a sloping roof surface to create usable space in the top floor or attic of a building by adding headroom. Example: Dalhousie Street, see Page 8	
Gable: the triangular portion of a wall between the edges of a sloping roof. **Jacobean Gable:** the gable extends above the roofline. Example: 1105 Dalhousie Street, see Page 7	
Hipped Roof: a roof where all sides slope downwards to the walls with no gables. Example: 273 Dalhousie Street, see Page 24	
Iron Cresting: A decorative ornament along the top of a roof. Iron cresting was popular in the Baroque era and also in Italianate, Victorian, Second Empire and Queen Anne styles of architecture. Example: 36 Sandwich Street South, see Page 49	

Palladian Window: a large window that is divided into three sections with the centre section larger than the two side sections and usually arched. Example: 495 Dalhousie Street, see Page 13	
Pediment: a triangular section above the horizontal structure (entablature), typically supported by columns. The inside of the triangle is called the tympanum. Example: 100 Sandwich Street South, Page 46	
Sidelight: a window, usually with a vertical emphasis, that flanks a door, and is often used to emphasize the importance of a primary entrance. **Transom Window:** the light above the doorway, also called a fanlight. Example: 210 Dalhousie Street, see Page 16	
Turret: a small tower that projects from the wall of a building. Example: 199 Dalhousie Street	
Vergeboard: also called bargeboards – hang from the projecting end of a roof and are often elaborately carved and ornamented. Example: 36 Sandwich Street South, Page 49	
Window Hood: A **hood** is the piece found above window openings, usually of an ornate design, and covers the top third of the opening. Hoods are commonly placed above arched or curved openings on both windows and doors. Example: Park Street, see Page 33	

Arts and Crafts: The overlying theme - the house was based on the function of the house. Rooms were oriented to take advantage of the movement of the sun for warmth and light during daylight hours. Side entrances allowed for useable space on the front facade for light or garden use. Arts and Crafts houses have many of these features: wood, stone or stucco siding; low-pitched roof; wide eaves with triangular brackets; exposed roof rafters; porch with thick square or round columns; stone porch supports; exterior chimney made with stone; open floor plans with few hallways; many windows, some with stained or leaded glass; beamed ceilings; dark wood wainscoting and moldings; built-in cabinets, shelves, and seating. Example: Dalhousie Street, see Page 13	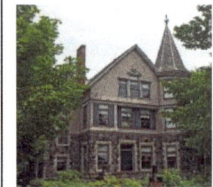
Georgian, before 1860 – This style began with the British King Georges in the 18th century. These buildings have balanced facades around a central door, medium-pitched gable roofs, and small paned windows. Example: 268 Dalhousie Street, see Page 23	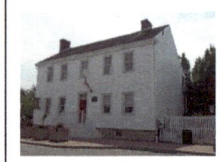
Gothic Revival, 1830-1890 – These decorative buildings have sharply-pitched gables with highly detailed verge boards, pointed-arch window openings, and dichromatic brickwork. It is a common style in Ontario. Example: 100 Sandwich Street South, Page 46	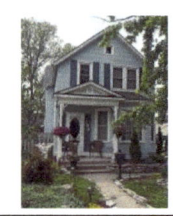

Classical Greek - For the three centuries after the sixth century B.C., the Greeks created monumental buildings with columns, pediments, entablatures, capitals, and bases. Example: Dalhousie Street, Page 9	
Palladian architecture is a European style of architecture derived from and inspired by the designs of the Venetian architect Andrea Palladio (1508–1580). Palladio's work was strongly based on the symmetry, perspective and values of the formal classical temple architecture of the Ancient Greeks and Romans. Example: 525 Dalhousie Street, see Page 11	
Queen Anne, 1885-1900 – This style is distinguished by an irregular outline featuring a combination of an offset tower, broad gables, projecting two-storey bays, verandahs, multi-sloped roofs, and tall, decorative chimneys. A mixture of brick and wood is common. Windows often have one large single-paned bottom sash and small panes in the upper sash. Example: 199 Dalhousie Street, Page 16	
Vernacular/Traditional Mode 1638 - 1950 Influenced but not defined by a particular style, vernacular buildings are made from easily available materials and exhibit local design characteristics. Example: 121 Sandwich Street South, Page 45	

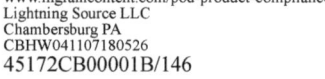